THE MOFFATS

Written by Eleanor Estes

Teacher Guide

MEMORIA PRESS
www.MemoriaPress.com

THE MOFFATS
Written by Eleanor Estes

TEACHER GUIDE
Contributing Editors: Leigh Lowe, Brenda Janke, Anne Parry, Brittany Mann

ISBN 978-1-61538-050-3

Cover illustration by Starr Steinbach

Contents

The Moffats

Appendix

PREPARING TO READ:

REVIEW

- Orally review any previous vocabulary.
- Review the plot of the book as read so far.
- Periodically review the concepts of character, setting, and plot.

STUDY GUIDE PREVIEW

- Reading Notes:
    - Read aloud together
    - This section gives the students key characters, places, terms that are relevant to a particular time period, etc.
- Vocabulary:
    - Read aloud together so that students will recognize words when they come across them in their reading.
- Comprehension Questions:
    - Read through these questions with students to encourage purposeful reading.

READING:

- Student reads the chapter (or selection of the chapter for that lesson) independently or to the teacher (for younger students).
- For younger students, you can alternate between teacher-read and student-read passages. Model good reading skills. Encourage students to read expressively and smoothly. Teacher may occasionally take oral reading grades.
- While reading, mark each vocabulary word as you come across it.
- Have students take note in their study guide margin of pages where a comprehension question is answered.

AFTER READING:

VOCABULARY

- Look at each word within the context that it is used, and help your students come up with the best synonym that defines the word. (Make sure students know the meaning of the synonym.)
- Record the word's meaning in the students' study guides. (Use students' knowledge of Latin and other vocabulary to decipher meanings.)

COMPREHENSION QUESTIONS

- Older students can answer these questions independently, but younger students (2nd-4th) need to answer the questions orally, form a good sentence, and then write it down, using correct punctuation, capitalization, and spelling. (You may want to write the sentence down for younger students after forming it orally, and then let students copy it perfectly.)
- It is not necessary to write the answer to every question. Some may be better answered orally.
- Answering questions and composing answers is a valuable learning activity. Questions require students to think; writing a concise answer is a good composition exercise.

QUOTATIONS AND DISCUSSION QUESTIONS

- Use the Quotations and Discussion Questions section of each lesson as a guide to your oral discussion of the key concepts in the chapter that may not be covered in the comprehension questions.
- These talking points can take your oral discussion to a higher level than covered in the students' written work. Use this time as an opportunity to introduce higher-level thinking. You can introduce concepts the students may not be mature enough to fully understand yet but that would be beneficial for them to begin thinking about.
- A key to the Discussion Questions is in the back of the Teacher Guide.

ENRICHMENT

- The Enrichment activities include composition, copywork, dictation, research, mapping, drawing, poetry work, literary terms, and more.
- This section has a variety of activities in it, but the most valuable activity is composition. Your students should complete at least one composition assignment each week. Proof students' work and have students copy composition until grammatically perfect. Insist on clear, concise writing. For younger students, start with 2-3 sentences, and do the assignment together. The students can form good sentences orally as you write them down, and then the students copy them.
- These activities can be completed as time and interest allow. Do not feel you need to complete all of these activities. Choose the ones that you feel are the best use of your students' time.

UNIT REVIEW AND TESTS

- There is a unit review and a quiz or test following every few lessons (varies by individual guide).
- On the weeks that have these reviews and tests, you may want to do the review early in the week, and then drill it orally a couple of times before giving the test at the end of the week.
- A final comprehensive test is also included.

Reading Notes

hitching post	a short post to which reigns of horses, mules, etc. are tied
trolley	a vehicle for public transportation that runs on tracks in the street
Druids	an ancient religious group in Britain, Ireland, and Gaul
bust	a dressmaker's dummy that serves as a model in place of a person

Vocabulary

1. She sprinkled sugar and cinnamon on the apples with the same **deft** fingers. nimble
2. When Mama went to town for **provisions** food; supplies
3. she got off the trolley, arms **laden** with bundles loaded down
4. count the cars … as they **galumphed** along. moved clumsily

Comprehension Questions

1. List each member of the Moffat family and give the age of each. The Moffat family consists of Mama, Sylvie (15), Joey (12), Jane (9), and Rufus (5 1/2).

2. Explain why the yellow house is the very best place to live on New Dollar Street. The yellow house sits in the middle of the curved street, and is the only house from which you can see both ends of the street.

Quotations

Jane clanked her feet against the hollow hitching post. For the hundredth time she was thinking that the yellow house was the best house to be living in in the whole block because it was the only house from which you could see all the way to both corners.

Discussion Questions

1. From your observations so far in the story, describe the main character, Jane.

Enrichment

Focus Passage: Copy the last paragraph on p. 5 (beginning with "'Come,' she said …" and ending with "brighter look." on the following page). Spelling, punctuation, and capitalization should be perfect.

Reading Notes

hitching post a short post to which reigns of horses, mules, etc. are tied
trolley a vehicle for public transportation that runs on tracks in the street
Druids an ancient religious group in Britain, Ireland, and Gaul
bust a dressmaker's dummy that serves as a model in place of a person

Vocabulary

1. She answered … with an **impertinent** grimace. rude; disrespectful
2. She could **impersonate** anyone. to mimic

Comprehension Questions

1. What is Mama's occupation? Who is Madame, and what purpose does she serve?

   Mama is a dressmaker; Madame is her "dummy," a model that can be adjusted and used to fit the size of any of Mama's clients.

2. What is the big news at the Moffats' house? Why is this happening?

   The owner of the house has decided to sell it because times are hard.

3. What is Jane's first reaction to the new sign? What thoughts help her adjust to this change?

   Jane is angry at first and doesn't believe the sign. Then she realizes that it is still the same house as before, and she hopes perhaps no one will actually buy it.

Quotations

"Maybe no one will have the money to buy the house," Jane whispered softly to Hildegarde. "You must remember these are hard times."

Discussion Questions

1. *What differences in daily activities and surroundings do you notice between the Moffats' life and your own?

   (Discussion questions that have a * are NECESSARY to discuss with students as they may appear on a test and are generally important in understanding the full flavor of the story.)

Enrichment

Setting: Using the descriptions given in this chapter, draw and label a map showing the location of the Moffats' house and its surroundings on New Dollar Street. Use the blank map page in the Appendix for your map.

Reading Notes

superintendent	a person who oversees and directs a district
delicatessen	"deli"; a shop that sells various goods, especially already prepared foods
ventriloquist	one who "throws" his voice so it sounds like it's coming from another source

Vocabulary

1. But she never walked *too* slowly lest she be arrested for **loitering**. standing idly
2. Obviously he was a person of great **dignity**. high importance; deserving respect
3. With these **ominous** words Peter Frost sounded his siren threatening

Comprehension Questions

1. How does Jane show respect toward Chief Mulligan when walking past his house?
   She is careful to stay off the grass, controls how she walks, doesn't allow Joe to ride his bike on the sidewalk or ring his bell, and prevents Rufus from leaving marks on the tar and driveway.

2. Who is the unfamiliar visitor on New Dollar Street? How does meeting him on the sidewalk affect Jane's day? Mr. Pennypepper, the new superintendent of schools, is the unfamiliar visitor. As he walks by her house, Jane follows him and mimics him. Peter Frost sees her and threatens to have her arrested for it.

3. Where is Jane's place of refuge when she is upset?
   She likes to sit inside the lilac bush in her yard.

Quotations

She strutted up the street right behind him. She stuck out her stomach and held up her head. She tried to copy his courteous air of friendly interest in all the houses and people as he glanced blandly from side to side. Janey had sneakers on her feet so she made no noise. The fine gentleman was totally unaware of the abbreviated shadow of himself that followed him up the street.

Discussion Questions

1. Using the descriptions from this chapter, add Chief Mulligan's house and Mr. Brooney's delicatessen to the map that you drew in the last chapter.

Enrichment

Focus Passage: Copy the fifth paragraph on p. 27 (beginning with "Jane looked around …"). Spelling, punctuation, and capitalization should be perfect.

Reading Notes

superintendent a person who oversees and directs a district
delicatessen "deli"; a shop that sells various goods, especially already prepared foods
ventriloquist one who "throws" his voice so it sounds like it's coming from another source

Vocabulary

1. With admirable **composure** he switched off his flashlight self-control
2. Jane **sauntered** nonchalantly into the house. leisurely strolled
3. Jane sauntered **nonchalantly** into the house. in a carefree or unconcerned manner

Comprehension Questions

1. Why does Jane end up spending hours in the bread box?

   She was hiding from the Chief of Police because she thought he was going to arrest her.

2. What three events prevent Jane from climbing out of the bread box?

   Mr. Brooney begins to sweep, Mrs. Shoemaker sits on the bread box while visiting with Mr. Brooney, and finally Jane falls asleep inside the box.

Quotations

"Little girl," he said, "don't you be afraid of a policeman anymore or of anything. Remember this. A policeman is for your protection. He's nothing to be scared of."

Discussion Questions

1. Jane had convinced herself that she could be arrested for irritating the Chief of Police. What do you think Mama would have said if Jane had told her about these fears? After she confessed her fears to him, how did the Chief's reaction change Jane's view of him?
2. Describe the event that led to Jane's discovery in the bread box.

Enrichment

Read the "Timeline of Interesting Events" in the Appendix.

1. What clues can you find in the first two chapters of *The Moffats* to show that the story takes place during the early 1900s?

Clues from Chapter 1: 1) "times are hard," no one is buying houses, and Dr. Witty has to sell the house because he needs the money. 2) Rufus is playing marbles. 3) The yellow house has a hitching post in front of it (used to tie up horses so they won't wander away when not being ridden). 4) Mama wonders what all the commotion is outside, and one of her guesses is that there might be an airplane in the sky. Planes were relatively new inventions and not often seen. 5) Mama wore a hat and gloves any time she left the house.

Clues from Chapter 2: 1) Rufus made a scooter out of an old roller skate and a soapbox. He couldn't buy one; he had to "make do." 2) Jane buys five pounds of sugar for her mother for only a quarter.

avg. cost is 68¢ / pound in USA in 2022

Reading Notes

hustle-bustle busy and noisy activity
an air of finality a tone indicating that no further discussion is needed
freighters trains used mainly for transporting cargo

Vocabulary

1. You don't want to grow up to be a **dunce**, do you? ignorant person
2. they started to drag him **ignominiously** in the right direction. disgracefully
3. Mud pies? he asked himself **sarcastically**. mockingly

Comprehension Questions

1. How does Rufus feel about going to school? Rufus is very excited about going to school. He has looked forward to it for a long time.

2. How does Hughie feel about going to school? Hughie dreads the idea of school. He howls and fights to keep from going, then runs away.

3. How do Mr. Pennypepper's instructions conflict with Mama's instructions? Mama had told Rufus to wait at school for Jane; she had also told the children never to go onto the railroad tracks. Mr. Pennypepper tells Rufus to bring Hughie back if he runs away from school. He wants Rufus to watch out for Hughie.

Quotations

Oh, he was enjoying himself hugely. All the new smells! First his new book, then the chalk dust whenever the teacher made lines on the board. And best of all this desk! All his own! Rufus liked it here.

Discussion Questions

1. Why did Rufus disobey his mother to follow Hughie? Did Rufus make a wise decision? How else might he have handled the situation?
2. Add the school and Nelly Cadwalader's house to your map.

Enrichment

Focus Passage: Copy the fifth paragraph on p. 39 (beginning with "Rufus and Jane walked hand in hand."). Spelling, punctuation, and capitalization should be perfect.

Reading Notes

hustle-bustle	busy and noisy activity
an air of finality	a tone indicating that no further discussion is needed
freighters	trains used mainly for transporting cargo

Vocabulary

1. regarded Hughie with a mixture of admiration and **contempt**. dislike, disapproval
2. Up top, on the **viaduct**, the trolley from Cranbury ran. bridge
3. soon they should be at the New Haven **depot**. train station

Comprehension Questions

1. What is Rufus' reaction when he realizes the train is actually moving? What is Hughie's reaction?

   Rufus is scared. He panics and wants to jump off the moving train. He also begins to recite his address as his mother has taught him to do if he got lost. Hughie happily watches the schoolhouse disappear, enjoying the ride.

2. What is the positive outcome from the boys' adventure?

   At the end of it all, they arrive safely back home, and Hughie decides he wants to go to school to learn to be an engineer someday.

Quotations

Goodness, this train was just speeding along. Of course, Rufus and Hughie couldn't stand too close to the engineer. But they could watch the fireman, and they saw enough to see that running an engine was a marvelous job.

Discussion Questions

1. Find the New York, New Haven, Hartford, Boston train route on a map. Where do you think the imaginary town of Cranbury might be located? You will need a map of the New York, Connecticut, and Massachusetts coastline. (Note p. 51, paragraph beginning, "The two boys looked back.")

Enrichment

Sequencing: Number the following sentences in correct order. Then copy them in paragraph form. Be sure to INDENT the first sentence!

__5__ At the next stop, New Haven, a trackman helped them board a train back to Cranbury.
__1__ Hughie Pudge refused to go to school.
__3__ When Hughie escaped, Rufus followed him into a train car.
__4__ Suddenly, the train began to move!
__6__ After arriving home, Hughie was willing to return to school.
__2__ Mr. Pennypepper gave Rufus the responsibility of keeping Hughie at school.

Reading Notes

Sunday school/catechism classes for religious instruction that meet on Sundays

Salvation Army a Christian organization focused on teaching the Bible and helping the poor

grade the slope of a hill

draught an alternate spelling for the word "draft," a current of air

Vocabulary

1. green grapes the rain and the wind had knocked off the **arbor** frame for growing vines
2. she stumbled and **groped** for the right words. searched blindly or uncertainly
3. **Unanimous** consent from Rufus and Jane. of one mind; in full agreement

Comprehension Questions

1. What alters the children's plan to go to Sunday School?

   The Salvation Army man asks for directions, and Joe decides they should ride with him to show him the way.

2. How do the Moffats justify their Sunday adventure as a good deed?

   They reason that the Salvation Army is just like Sunday school, and if they help this man they will avoid arriving late to Sunday school.

3. How do the children try to get word to their mother?

   They write a message to Sylvie on the drinking trough with chalk.

Quotations

Up Shingle Hill in a horse and wagon! Many were the times they had plodded wearily up that steep hill on foot to pick violets, or goldenrod and asters. Now up, up the horse drew the light wagon and the three children and the sleeping man.

Discussion Questions

1. How did Rufus learn sections of the catechism, Latin, and history? Have you ever learned something in a similar manner?
2. Research more information about the Salvation Army. Have its activities changed over the years?

Enrichment

Focus Passage: Copy the second paragraph on p. 65 (beginning with "You know the way through town ..."). Spelling, punctuation, and capitalization should be perfect.

Reading Notes

Sunday school/catechism classes for religious instruction that meet on Sundays

Salvation Army a Christian organization focused on teaching the Bible and helping the poor

grade the slope of a hill

draught an alternate spelling for the word "draft," a current of air

Vocabulary

1. "Is this Orchard Grove?" he asked **incredulously**. in disbelief
2. They were too **engrossed** with … driving a real horse focused; absorbed
3. No wonder they all looked pretty **subdued** quiet; restrained

Comprehension Questions

1. How do the children lose the sleeping Captain? They cut a corner too sharply with the wagon and drive into the ditch. This bounces the Captain out the back onto the road, but they don't hear him shout for help.

2. What causes the children to realize the Captain is gone? They no longer hear him snoring.

3. How did their message on the drinking trough actually confuse matters later on? The rain had washed away only part of the message, and Sylvie couldn't figure out what it meant.

Quotations

The horse galloped into the shed and came snorting to a stop just as the heavens opened and let down such a rain as had not fallen before that summer. The wind tore branches from the trees. The thunder cracked like a giant whip and lightning sizzled through the air.

Discussion Questions

1. Discuss the imagery of the quote above. How do the words the author chose give you a vivid picture of the storm?

Enrichment

Dictation: Listen carefully as your teacher reads aloud. As he/she reads, write down what you hear. Pay close attention to spelling, capitalization, and punctuation. When finished, compare your paragraph to the book, and circle any errors.

Dictate (from last paragraph, p. 73): Joe, Jane, and Rufus didn't look back. None of them looked back once on the scene of their near disaster. If they had, they might have seen the Captain sprawled on the ground along with piles of newspapers. That last lurch out of the ditch had sent him flying out of the wagon into the ditch.

Reading Notes

hobyahs, pookas, goblins, hobgoblins mischievous spirits in folklore

attic hatch an opening in the attic floor that serves as an entrance from below

"G-R-I-N-D your bones" a reference to the giant's threat in "Jack and the Beanstalk"

Vocabulary

1. Miss Partridge was so **amiable**. friendly; good natured
2. Now don't be **gallivanting** through the streets wandering about

Comprehension Questions

1. List some of the grudges and complaints the Moffats have against Peter Frost. (Note how the illustrator portrays them.) Peter pulls Sylvie's curls, made Rufus fall off the hitching post, tricked Jane and put sand in her mouth, and scared Jane into thinking she could be arrested for mimicking someone.
2. Who had lived in the yellow house before the Moffats? What was his occupation? Dr. Witty had lived in the house. He was a dentist.
3. What plan is devised to "even the score" with Peter? What props are used? The Moffats plan to create a "ghost" in the attic to scare him. They use Madame, white sheets, a jack-o-lantern head, human teeth, a flashlight, and a rope.

Quotations

They stuck the teeth in the pumpkin head, and at last it was finished. They looked at their work with satisfaction. Phew! She looked gruesome, particularly with that old mare's tooth hanging over her lower lip.

Discussion Questions

1. Explain the difference between Miss Partridge and Mr. Allgood. Which teacher did the students prefer? Why?

Enrichment

Focus Passage: Copy the three paragraphs of dialogue on the bottom of p. 88 (beginning with "Jane grabbed the gingerbread ..." and ending with "scare Peter Frost."). Spelling, punctuation, and capitalization should be perfect.

Reading Notes

hobyahs, pookas, goblins, hobgoblins	mischievous spirits in folklore
attic hatch	an opening in the attic floor that serves as an entrance from below
"G-R-I-N-D your bones"	a reference to the giant's threat in "Jack and the Beanstalk"

Vocabulary

1. Oh, his arrogance was **insufferable.** intolerable
2. out of the night came … a howl of **reproach.** disapproval
3. he **blanched** visibly when again … came the same wild howl. whitened by color being removed
4. Madame-the-ghost started **careening** madly toward them. moving uncontrollably
5. the place sounded like **bedlam.** total confusion

Comprehension Questions

1. What is stored in the attic? Many stuffed wild animals and birds belonging to Dr. Witty are stored there.
2. What clues indicate to Mama that the children had been pranksters while she was out? She saw Peter racing away, frightened, and she sees the cat behaving strangely, and Madame wearing the dress backward.

Quotations

But he stopped short, for out of the night came a long-drawn howl, a howl of reproach.

Discussion Questions

1. What happened in the attic to scare Peter Frost? In what ways did the Moffats frighten themselves as much as they frightened Peter?
2. Read the English fairy tale "Jack and the Beanstalk." Why do you think the events in the attic made Rufus think of this story?

Enrichment

Personification: to give human characteristics to a thing or idea.

Example: The water defied the cold.

Circle the noun that is being personified. Underline the words that show human characteristics.

1. Mr. Pennypepper's walk proclaimed, without a doubt, that he was a very important man.
2. The light from the kitchen spread a warm welcome to them.
3. The bread box held her a silent prisoner for what seemed a very long time.
4. A hatch… fell open with a groan and the strange musty smell of the attic greeted them.
5. The thunder cracked its mighty whip across the sky as the lightning sped through the air.
6. The engine of the Bay State Express was just itching to be off.
7. The freighters in the train yard beckoned to him invitingly until he could resist no longer.
8. The longer she stared at it the louder the sign screamed that this was no longer her house.
9. The leaves fairly danced across the page of Jane's autumn drawing.
10. Madame could impersonate anyone.

Reading Notes

sailor's hornpipe	a dance that imitates a sailor's life and duties on a ship; used as an exercise
"Master" Joseph Moffat	a formal title of address for a boy or young man
encore	used by an audience in calling for an additional performance
impromptu	unplanned

Vocabulary

1. He knew though that **remonstrance** was useless. protest; bargain
2. She said all the charms she knew to **avert** rain to avoid
3. Jane … wound one of her straggling locks around her fingers in **pensive** silence. thoughtful
4. Sylvie ran the hairbrush hastily and **belligerently** over Jane's hair aggressively

Comprehension Questions

1. What arrangement was made between Mama and Miss Chichester? Miss Chichester teaches Mama's children to dance in exchange for the dresses Mama makes her.

2. How does each child feel about dancing lessons? Sylvie loves them and has a natural talent; Jane likes to imagine herself as a graceful dancer, but actually isn't very good; Joe dislikes lessons very much and isn't any good.

Quotations

Mama knew he didn't like parties, dancing school, speaking pieces. Still she thought he should do these things. "You must learn to be graceful and to have nice manners even though you are a boy," she said.

Discussion Questions

1. In what way is the special arrangement of the Moffats' dancing lessons related to the setting of the story?
2. The author tells us that Joe hated parties and dancing and found every way he could to avoid learning, even while in dance class. What evidence do you see in this chapter that, despite his disinterest, Joe is still actually learning how to dance?

Enrichment

Focus Passage: Copy the last section of dialogue on p. 111 (beginning with "As if in answer to her thoughts ..." and ending in the middle of the last paragraph with "in pensive silence."). Spelling, punctuation, and capitalization should be perfect.

Reading Notes

sailor's hornpipe	a dance that imitates a sailor's life and duties on a ship; used as an exercise
"Master" Joseph Moffat	a formal title of address for a boy or young man
encore	used by an audience in calling for an additional performance
impromptu	unplanned

Vocabulary

1. Joe became in a moment the most **morose** and melancholy of creatures. gloomy; sullen
2. Chester Pudge … was to perform … in his own **inimitable** fashion defying imitation; matchless

Comprehension Questions

1. What was supposed to be Joe's assignment on recital day? What changes this?

   Joe was supposed to seat the audience and turn pages for the pianist. When Chet Pudge doesn't show up, Miss Chichester tells Joe he will have to perform the sailor's hornpipe.

2. Why was the sailor's hornpipe the most praised routine in the recital?

   The audience was very enthusiastic about seeing the little dog dance with Joe.

Quotations

Joe was so startled by the new development that he paused, hoping this was to be deliverance from this miserable dance. Then he realized that the dog, Sugar, was doing the sailor's hornpipe and was looking to him for cues. Gee, what a smart dog*, thought Joe enthusiastically, and took up the steps again. Bow and kick! Shuffle and stamp! The two got on together with perfect understanding.*

Discussion Questions

1. Why did Joe begin to enjoy the dance partway through his performance?
2. Why did Joe leave the performance whistling, even though he did not get the promised ten cents?
3. Have you ever had to perform for an audience when you felt unprepared? How did you feel?

Enrichment

Character Identification: Write the name of the character that each phrase describes.

1. Mama ______ works as a seamstress for a living
2. Jane ______ likes to look at things the upside-down way
3. Madame ______ used as a model for Mama's customers
4. Chief Mulligan ______ laughed so hard that tears ran into his whiskers
5. Mr. Pennypepper ______ nods politely to everyone he passes
6. Peter Frost ______ an insufferable bully
7. Hughie Pudge ______ decided to become an engineer when he grows up
8. Captain of Salvation Army ______ could only be awakened by the beat of a drum
9. Mr. Allgood ______ causes the children to sit as straight as ramrods
10. Miss Chichester ______ told Joe his impromptu performance made a success of the recital

Elements of Literature: Writing sentences about the story.

Character

Character means <u>who</u> is in the story.

1. Write one sentence describing one of the members of the Moffat family. ____________

   Answers will vary.

2. Write one sentence describing a character who is not a member of the Moffat family. ____________

   Answers will vary.

Setting

Setting means the <u>time</u> and <u>place</u> in which the story happens.

1. Write one sentence about the setting of the story. ____________

   Answers will vary.

2. Write one descriptive sentence about a place familiar to the Moffat children. ____________

   Answers will vary.

Plot

Plot means <u>action</u> or <u>what happens</u> in the story.

1. Write at least three sentences explaining what happened between Jane and the Chief of Police. Refer to Chapter 2 to find descriptive details for your sentences.

   Answers will vary.

Drawing Page

Illustrate the character in the Moffat family that you described on the previous page.

Vocabulary

Write the letter of the vocabulary word on the line in front of its definition.

1. _n_ aggressively		a. nonchalantly
2. _h_ in disbelief		b. contempt
3. _g_ food; supplies		c. depot
4. _k_ not able to be imitated		d. subdued
5. _p_ in full agreement		e. pensive
6. _t_ moving uncontrollably		f. arbor
7. _l_ sad		g. provisions
8. _r_ leisurely strolled		h. incredulously
9. _c_ train station		i. laden
10. _d_ quiet; restrained		j. viaduct
11. _s_ threatening		k. inimitable
12. _i_ loaded down		l. melancholy
13. _b_ dislike; disapproval		m. impersonate
14. _f_ frame for growing vines		n. belligerently
15. _e_ thoughtful		o. impertinent
16. _a_ in a carefree or unconcerned manner		p. unanimous
17. _m_ to mimic		q. deft
18. _o_ rude; disrespectful		r. sauntered
19. _q_ nimble		s. ominous
20. _j_ bridge		t. careening

Short Answer

Answer the following questions in complete sentences.

1. List two differences in activities and surroundings that you have noticed between the Moffats' life and your own.

   Possible answers: Rufus plays marbles, an airplane flying overhead is an unusual event, Jane knits, they have a potbellied stove, Mama makes dresses for a living, the For Sale sign is nailed directly to the house, the hitching post, trolleys are a common way to travel.

2. How did Mr. Pennypepper's instructions to Rufus conflict with Mama's instructions?

   Mama had told Rufus to wait at school for Jane; she had also told the children never to go onto the railroad tracks. Mr. Pennypepper told Rufus to bring Hughie back if he ran away from school. He wanted Rufus to watch out for Hughie.

3. List two grudges the Moffats had against Peter Frost.

   Peter pulls Sylvie's curls, he made Rufus fall off the hitching post, he tricked Jane and put sand in her mouth, and he scared Jane into thinking she could be arrested for mimicking someone.

4. Who lived in the yellow house before the Moffats? What was his occupation?

   Dr. Witty had lived in the house. He was a dentist.

5. How did Sylvie, Jane, and Joe each feel about dancing lessons?

   Sylvie: Sylvie loved her dance lessons and had a natural talent for it.

   Jane: Jane liked to imagine herself as a graceful dancer, but she really wasn't a good dancer.

   Joe: Joe disliked the lessons very much, wasn't any good, and tried to avoid them.

Reading Notes

mustard plaster, castor oil, camomile tea	home remedies used to treat sickness
scarlet fever	a contagious disease, marked by a red rash, high fever, and inflamed throat
hurdy-gurdy man	a street musician who earns a living by playing a hand-cranked organ
brougham	a four-wheeled, boxlike, closed carriage that seats two to four people

Vocabulary

1. Then she lit the **feeble** gas jet ______ weak ______
2. Feeling excited over all this **unaccustomed** responsibility ______ unusual ______
3. I'll tack the scarlet fever **quarantine** sign on the house. ______ enforced isolation ______
4. Sylvie, Joe, and Janey looked at Mama in **consternation**. ______ concern; worry ______
5. there was a little **consolation** in that thought, but it didn't ease the worry ______ comfort ______

Comprehension Questions

1. What is the second sign on the yellow house? Why is it put there? ______

   The second sign is the scarlet fever quarantine sign. It warns people to avoid the house as a way of keeping the disease from spreading to other people and homes in the community.

2. What is one positive thing about the new sign on the door? ______

   As long as the quarantine sign is on the door, no one will come to buy the house.

Quotations

"Well, anyway," she said, "at least we will not have to worry about moving for a while. No one will think of buying the yellow house while there is a scarlet fever sign on the door."

Who said this? ______ Mama ______ To whom? ______ the children ______

Discussion Questions

1. Read Hans Christian Andersen's fairy tale, *The Little Match Girl.* Explain why Jane identified with this story. (One version of this story can be found in the Appendix.)

Enrichment

Focus Passage: Copy the first complete paragraph on p. 125 (beginning with "When he had gone …"). Spelling, punctuation, and capitalization should be perfect.

Melody on pg 78 Story on pg 76-77

Reading Notes

mustard plaster, castor oil, camomile tea	home remedies used to treat sickness
scarlet fever	a contagious disease, marked by a red rash, high fever, and inflamed throat
hurdy-gurdy man	a street musician who earns a living by playing a hand-cranked organ
brougham	a four-wheeled, boxlike, closed carriage that seats two to four people

Vocabulary

1. she jumped up and ran under the stove with **disdainful** hisses. scornful
2. But now Rufus was beginning to **recuperate**. to recover; to get better

Comprehension Questions

1. How does the family work together during Rufus' illness? Mama constantly cares for Rufus. They both remained separated from the rest of the family. The other children become responsible for all the daily household chores, such as cooking, cleaning, warming flatirons, and keeping the fire going.

2. How is Rufus amused during his time of illness?

   Mother tells him fairy tales and stories about her childhood in New York.

Quotations

Mama had a hard time keeping him amused. She told him stories. She told him the kind that always begins, "Once upon a time ..." and she told him the kind about when she was a little girl in New York, that always began, "Well, then ..." or just, "Well ..."

Discussion Questions

1. *List some specific differences between how illness was treated in the Moffats' time compared to today's methods.
2. Look in the Appendix for the song "Daisy Bell." What is another name for a bicycle-built-for-two?
3. What other fictitious or real people do you know that were affected by scarlet fever?

Enrichment

Dictation: Listen carefully as your teacher reads aloud. As he/she reads, write down what you hear. Pay close attention to spelling, capitalization, and punctuation. When finished, compare your paragraph to the book, and circle any errors.

Dictate (from first full paragraph, p. 125): When he had gone, Jane felt more lonely and sad than ever. Seeing him light his matches had made her think of "The Little Match Girl." Great tears welled in her eyes, some for Rufus, some for the cold lamplighter, some for herself …

Reading Notes

Flexible Flyer sled	a wooden sled made of slats and steel runners; invented in 1889
chilblains	swelling of the hands and feet due to cold weather
mackintosh	a waterproof raincoat; invented in 1836 by Charles Mackintosh
coal scuttle	a metal bucket, with a lip, used to hold and carry coal

Vocabulary

1. I can't **abide** to look at those oranges any longer. stand
2. The two stood there in front of the coal man in the utmost **dejection**. low spirits
3. They were so **dismayed** they could say nothing. disappointed; distressed
4. They stood **disconsolately** for some seconds cheerlessly

Comprehension Questions

1. In what ways do the Moffats try to save money? Jane puts cardboard inside her shoe where the sole has worn away. Joe sifts through the ashes to find lumps of coal they can reburn. Mama manages the money very carefully, and she tells Joe to count the change carefully.

2. What are some circumstances that make things financially difficult for the Moffats? Rufus had been sick and Mama hadn't been able to work. The ladies in town are not buying as many dresses, and when they do, they often buy them from a store.

3. What happens at the coal barge the first time? Joe can't find the money, so the man won't give them any coal.

Quotations

Jane looked at him in helpless horror. The man stood there like a rock and said nothing. Joe gulped. In all his pockets, nothing! Could he have lost it? Lost all the money they had?

Discussion Questions

1. Why did the Moffats need coal? What is a coal barge?

Enrichment

Focus Passage: Copy the sixth complete paragraph on p. 138 (beginning with "The Moffats were feeling …"). Spelling, punctuation, and capitalization should be perfect.

Reading Notes

Flexible Flyer sled	a wooden sled made of slats and steel runners; invented in 1889
chilblains	swelling of the hands and feet due to cold weather
mackintosh	a waterproof raincoat; invented in 1836 by Charles Mackintosh
coal scuttle	a metal bucket, with a lip, used to hold and carry coal

Vocabulary

1. "Lost the money!" repeated Sylvie, **aghast**. shocked; dismayed
2. a black space where the water still **defied** the cold. stubbornly resisted

Comprehension Questions

1. What is Mama's reaction to the news that they'd lost the money to buy coal?

   She is silent at first, then tries to make the best of it.

2. How is their problem resolved?

   Joe and Jane search for the money all the way home, and then Joe finds it on the mantle when they get there. Then they go back to the coal yard to buy the coal.

Quotations

As the man shoveled the coal into the bag again, the children walked to the edge of the wharf. The harbor looked as though it were frozen tight. But far out they could see a black space where the water still defied the cold.

Discussion Questions

1. List some advantages to the Moffats' simpler lifestyle.

Enrichment

Personification: to give human characteristics to a thing or idea.

Example: The water defied the cold.

Circle the noun that is being personified. Underline the words that show human characteristics.

1. But the wind was now on their backs and urged them up the street swiftly.
2. The wind laid giant palms on their backs and tried to hurry them along.
3. The wind had tossed aside its mantle of clouds for a time.
4. In her imagination Jane's feet carefully followed each step of the dance with graceful ease.
5. The carpet sweeper found its own way across the floor as Jane read on, lost in the story of "The Little Match Girl."
6. The wind tried to snatch their hats from their heads.
7. Somehow or other her feet marched her right over to the ice-cream counter.
8. Madame was on the porch wearing a rather disapproving air.
9. The rooms were empty, but they wore a look of expectancy.
10. Fingers and coins parted company reluctantly.

Reading Notes

wooden horse of Troy	a reference to the Trojan horse in Virgil's epic poem, *The Aeneid*
game of beast, bird, or fish	a word guessing game that is an early version of Hangman
Dresden shepherd	a collectible china figurine imported from Dresden, Germany
"with bated breath"	in great suspense

Vocabulary

1. because of the graceful way … he **cantered** up the street. galloped
2. He stood there **immobile**. not able to move
3. The shingles **protruded** over each window extended
4. like **languorous**, drooping eyelids. still; sleepy

Comprehension Questions

1. After watching Jane from inside, why does Mama send her on an errand? What is the errand?

   Mama wants to get Jane's mind off the horse so that she wouldn't walk under it again! Her errand is to deliver a sleeve to Tilly Cadwalader.

2. What is the Moffats' code about sharing? How does Jane break it? How does that make her feel?

   Their code is "share and share alike." Jane breaks this code by spending her entire nickel on herself. Afterwards she feels ashamed and angry with herself. She can't even enjoy the cone.

Quotations

Share and share alike was the rule of the Moffat household, and no one ever thought to dispute it.

Discussion Questions

1. *List examples from the book of Jane's overactive imagination.

Enrichment

Focus Passage: Copy the first complete paragraph on p. 162 (beginning with "But here she was at Brooney's."). Spelling, punctuation, and capitalization should be perfect.

Reading Notes

wooden horse of Troy	a reference to the Trojan horse in Virgil's epic poem, *The Aeneid*
game of beast, bird, or fish	a word guessing game that is an early version of Hangman
Dresden shepherd	a collectible china figurine imported from Dresden, Germany
"with bated breath"	in great suspense

Vocabulary

1. this kitten was the most **enterprising** of the four. adventurous
2. You must call as **fervently** for this one as that one. passionately; zealously

Comprehension Questions

1. Describe the "choosing game." Each kitten is placed by itself in the center of the room. The children sit in four separate corners of the room, each calling enthusiastically to the kitten. The kitten "belongs" to whichever child it walks towards.

2. Why does Jane have mixed feelings about the kitten she wins? She feels she doesn't deserve the best kitten because she had behaved so selfishly with the ice cream.

Quotations

But the more she ate, the less she enjoyed it. She was a pig, that's what, a pig.

To whom does this refer? Jane What is she eating? an ice cream cone

Discussion Questions

1. What were some of the other things Jane could have bought with her nickel? What can a nickel buy now?

Enrichment

Sequencing: Number the following sentences in correct order. Then copy them in paragraph form. Be sure to INDENT the first sentence!

__2__ After delivering the dress sleeve, Tilly gave Jane a nickel as a means of saying thank you.
__4__ There were many choices, but she allowed herself to be tempted into buying ice cream.
__1__ Jane's mother sent her on an errand to the Cadwalader's to get her mind off of horses.
__5__ Jane felt unbearably guilty and ashamed knowing her decision had been selfish.
__3__ The money seemed to burn in her pocket as she thought how to spend it.
__6__ Later that afternoon she won Boots, the kitten, although she knew she didn't deserve it.

Reading Notes

Nubian desert a desert made mostly of a sandy plateau in northeast Sudan, Africa
Houdini a magician, escape artist, and stunt performer
hypnotize a means of controlling another's mind/actions by the use of repeated words

Vocabulary

1. they had a way of appearing ... at most **inopportune** moments. inconvenient
2. In **exasperation** Mama finally put on her gloves extreme annoyance, frustration
3. Now they assumed a **martyred** air greatly pained or tormented
4. That **evoking** no response, she would ... knock. bringing about
5. sometimes she would ... peer **intently** within. with great focus

Comprehension Questions

1. Who are the Murdocks and how do they become involved with the Moffats?
The Murdock family first notices the yellow house when Jane is cleaning mud off the For Sale sign. They are considering buying the house, so they keep returning to look at it.

2. What are several things about the Murdocks that annoy the Moffats?
They drop in unannounced, pick the fruit, climb on the roof, peer down the chimney, walk around the yard, sit in the swing, wander inside and out, ask endless questions, and measure for electrical outlets.

3. Why is Letitia particularly irritating to the Moffats? She climbs the ladder, raps on the windows, knocks on the door, rings the doorbell, and peeks in the windows. She is very persistent.

Quotations

For instance, take the Murdocks. Of all those who had come to look at the house so far, the Murdocks were easily the most difficult to endure.

Discussion Questions

1. A family sometimes has to move from a house that is familiar and dear to them. Why would that be difficult? How might it affect various members of the family?

Enrichment

Focus Passage: Copy the second complete paragraph on p. 171 (beginning with "'Look!' they would say."). Spelling, punctuation, and capitalization should be perfect.

Reading Notes

Nubian desert a desert made mostly of a sandy plateau in northeast Sudan, Africa
Houdini a magician, escape artist, and stunt performer
hypnotize a means of controlling another's mind/actions by the use of repeated words

Vocabulary

1. When on occasion she did manage to outwit her **adversaries** enemies; competitors
2. marched with solemn **mien** around the yard manner; appearance
3. She then began to chant in **sepulchral** (suh-**puhl**-kruhl) tones gloomy; dismal

Comprehension Questions

1. What gets Jane's attention while playing outdoors? How does it influence her play?

   An airplane gets Jane's attention as she hears it flying overhead. Airplanes are fairly rare, and seeing one is exciting for her. Jane wishes she could fly, but since she cannot, she pretends her doll Hildegard can fly. But as she sends her doll soaring in the sky, it lands with a crash and breaks!

2. How does Jane finally rid the house of Letitia?

   She pretends to hypnotize Rufus, who attacks her like a dog and chases her away.

Quotations

Letitia's feelings never seemed in the least hurt by the Moffats' refusal to open the door to her. She entered into the whole thing as in a game, which might be called, "Trying-to-get-into-the-yellow-house." When on occasion she did manage to outwit her adversaries and actually gained entrance in the yellow house, she would scream triumphantly, "I got in!"

Discussion Questions

1. Research Harry Houdini. When did he live? What were some of his famous escapist acts?

Enrichment

Dictation: Listen carefully as your teacher reads aloud. As he/she reads, write down what you hear. Pay close attention to spelling, capitalization, and punctuation. When finished, compare your paragraph to the book, and circle any errors.

Dictate (from fourth paragraph, p. 183): With this, Rufus fell to his knees, began to frisk about and bark. He enjoyed acting like a dog so much that his barks became more and more furious. He started nosing at Letitia's heels. He sounded like all the dogs of New Dollar Street, chasing and barking after a motorcycle.

Reading Notes

row a clamorous quarrel

without a leg to stand on an idiom meaning "having no support for one's argument"

Vocabulary

1. although he still felt somewhat **reluctant**. unwilling
2. A **baleful** look came over his face threatening harm

Comprehension Questions

1. What are the children's plans for the first day of summer vacation? They plan to take a picnic and spend the day at the beach.

2. How do the Moffats end up on the trolley? Whose idea is it? Why? It is Rufus' idea; Rufus wants to ride the trolley to learn about being a motorman. Jane convinces Joe to ride with him.

Quotations

It used to be such a long walk over to Sandy Beach. So long that Rufus used to have to be dragged half the way in his express wagon, he'd get so tired. But now it was nothing to get there. The new Second Avenue trolley line whisked you there in just no time at all. If you were lucky, that is, and the motorman did not have to wait at the switch for the trolley that was coming from the other direction to get past him.

Discussion Questions

1. Why did the children pick out the tinfoil from the empty cigarette cases and gum wrappers?
2. When Rufus boarded the trolley, the driver assumed he was not yet five years old and said he did not need to pay. What was Rufus' response to this surprise? Was it the best response? Why or why not?

Enrichment

Focus Passage: Copy the third complete paragraph on p. 187 (beginning with "Five cents apiece!"). Spelling, punctuation, and capitalization should be perfect.

Reading Notes

row a clamorous quarrel
without a leg to stand on an idiom meaning "having no support for one's argument"

Vocabulary

1. The others … roused out of their **lethargy** laziness
2. The others … **implored** him to stop. urgently begged
3. So the passengers all ran … from what looked like an **inevitable** crash. unavoidable
4. trying by **emphatic** waves of the arms to indicate what they meant forceful; urgent
5. like great **tawny** tigers at bay. yellow
6. And he edged his car an inch nearer, **menacingly**. threateningly

Comprehension Questions

1. What excitement is encountered on the trolley? Two trolleys run in opposite directions on the same track, and one is supposed to wait for the other to complete its run. However, the motorman driving the Moffats' trolley decides to confront the other motorman and there is almost a crash as the two trolleys meet on the track.

2. How do the children react to the adventure? They think it is very exciting and nothing else they could do that day would match it. They can't wait to tell Mama.

Quotations

Such a thing was unheard of! Two trolleys on the same track, one going north, the other going south, could do only one thing—meet with a crash.

Discussion Questions

1. How would you describe each of the two trolley motormen? Use plenty of descriptive detail.

Enrichment

Character Identification: Write the name of the character that each phrase describes.

1. Dr. Belknap — a good, jolly man who diagnoses Rufus' scarlet fever
2. Tilly Cadwalader — the eldest and only girl in her family that wears her hair high on her head
3. Boots — shows marks of personality that lift her above the usual run of cats and kittens
4. Letitia Murdock — would ring and ring the doorbell, then run around to the back door and knock
5. old McCann — an old man with a walrus mustache who takes driving a trolley car very seriously
6. O'Brien — wears his hat tipped on the back of his head and sits all slouchy on his stool
7. Jane — was a pig, that's what, a pig
8. Rufus — wanted to ride the trolley to see the business about the red lights
9. Joe — practices his stilt-walking in the backyard
10. Sylvie — spends the first week of her summer vacation at Camp Lincoln

Reading Notes

tenants people who rent a dwelling from the owner of the building

grate a framework of crossed metal bars for holding coal for burning

Vocabulary

1. But there was also a feeling of **expectancy** and excitement. anticipation; suspense
2. Rufus **shinned** up the cherry tree climbed, using hands and legs for gripping

Comprehension Questions

1. What are some of the memories the Moffats have in the yellow house? All of Rufus' memories are there since he has lived there all his life. Jane made paper dolls, studied, explored, and dreamed. They all climbed trees, played baseball and cops and robbers, walked fences, and raced the trolley cars on the street.

2. Describe how the Moffats' new house is different from the yellow house. The new house is smaller with a huge front yard and a small backyard. It has few trees and only one arbor. However, they know that eventually there might be many things they will like.

3. Why does moving make Jane think of Sylvie growing up? Moving makes Jane realize that time passes and people change as they grow up. She can see some changes already in Sylvie and pictures her getting married and leaving home.

Quotations

So this was the last, the very last day in the yellow house. No wonder everybody was going around with a lump in his throat. But there was also a feeling of expectancy and excitement.

Discussion Questions

1. What did each of the Moffat children do "one last time" on the last day in the yellow house? Why do you think they felt they needed to do these things?
2. How did Jane look at the new house? When has she done this before? What was she looking at then? Why does she like to look at things this way?

Enrichment

Focus Passage: Copy the last five paragraphs of dialogue on p. 198 (beginning with "'It's gone!' screamed Jane" through "Those Murdocks!"). Spelling, punctuation, and capitalization should be perfect.

Reading Notes

tenants people who rent a dwelling from the owner of the building

grate a framework of crossed metal bars for holding coal for burning

Vocabulary

1. This house … seemed neither friendly nor unfriendly, just **indifferent**. unconcerned; uninterested
2. "I'm not crying," denied Jane **indignantly**. with annoyance or resentment
3. These were bound **fast** to the wagon with thick ropes. tightly
4. In her hand were sprigs … she would **transplant** in the new yard. move and re-plant
5. She **skulked** along the house and then along the fence moved stealthily; lurked
6. there she sat, **glowering**. scowling

Comprehension Questions

1. What are some of the things Jane does to try to prepare herself for living in the new house? Do they help her? She looks at the new house the upside down way to get a different perspective. She looks at the empty rooms. She pretends she is coming home from school to see how that feels. No, they don't help. She thinks the house feels indifferent.

2. What makes Jane excited to move to the new house? She meets Nancy who lives in the house across the backyard fence. Nancy says she would like to be best friends with Jane!

Quotations

She caught her breath. A girl about her own age was sitting on a high branch of the tree. It was her hair that made Jane catch her breath. A head of tangled curls of gold just like the ones she herself had in her dreams.

Discussion Questions

1. The end of something is often memorable and can create emotional responses. Can you think of a "last chapter" in your life? How did you feel? What did you learn from the experience?
2. In this chapter Jane recited lines from R. L. Stevenson's poem "The Wind." Read the poem in the Appendix and memorize it.

Enrichment

Composition: Write a 5-sentence paragraph about your favorite character in *The Moffats.* Include an introductory sentence and a concluding sentence. When describing the character, use your book for details. Then explain **why** you like this character best.

Answers will vary.

Elements of Literature: Writing sentences about the story.

Character

Character means who is in the story.

1. Write one sentence describing Letitia Murdock. ______________________________

____

2. Write one sentence describing Boots the kitten. ______________________________

____

Setting

Setting means the time and place in which the story happens.

1. Write one descriptive sentence about the Moffats' new house. ______________________

____

____

Plot

Plot means action or what happens in the story.

1. Write at least three sentences describing what happened on the Second Avenue trolley. Refer to Chapter 11 to find descriptive details for your sentences. ______________________

____

____

____

____

____

____

2. Write two sentences about your favorite chapter in the book. Illustrate the events on the next page.

____

____

____

Storyboard

Vocabulary

Write the letter of the vocabulary word on the line in front of its definition.

1. __g__ stubbornly resisted
2. __k__ comfort
3. __i__ galloped
4. __q__ unconcerned; uninterested
5. __p__ extended
6. __o__ unavoidable
7. __c__ threateningly
8. __t__ scowling
9. __f__ passionately; zealously
10. __b__ weak
11. __m__ with great focus
12. __d__ scornful
13. __j__ not able to move
14. __h__ urgently begged
15. __n__ inconvenient
16. __e__ low spirits
17. __l__ still; sleepy
18. __s__ shocked; dismayed
19. __r__ yellow
20. __a__ enemies; competitors

a. adversaries
b. feeble
c. menacingly
d. disdainful
e. dejection
f. fervently
g. defied
h. implored
i. cantered
j. immobile
k. consolation
l. languorous
m. intently
n. inopportune
o. inevitable
p. protruded
q. indifferent
r. tawny
s. aghast
t. glowering

Short Answer

Answer the following questions in complete sentences.

1. Give one example of how illness was treated differently in the Moffats' time compared to today's methods.

   Some specific differences would be that the Moffats were quarantined in the house, the doctor visited Rufus in their home rather than at his office, and a grocery boy came to their house to deliver groceries.

2. Describe two ways the Moffats tried to save money.

   Jane put cardboard inside her shoe where the sole had worn away. Joe sifted through the ashes to find lumps of coal they could reburn. Mama was managing the money very carefully, and she told Joe to count the change carefully.

3. Describe one example of Jane's overactive imagination. Give details.

   Ch.2 - While in the bread box she pictured herself as a princess locked in a cavern.
   Ch.5 - Jane was frightened by the ghost she helped to build.
   Ch.6 - She imagined herself to be a graceful dancer.
   Ch.7 - She imagined she was the Little Match Girl.
   Ch.9 - She imagined the horse had wings, was the wooden horse of Troy, and was a bridge.

4. What excitement was encountered on the trolley?

   Two trolleys ran in opposite directions on the same track, and one was supposed to wait for the other to complete its run. However, the motorman driving the Moffats' trolley decided to confront the other motorman, and there was almost a crash as the two trolleys met on the track.

5. Describe how the Moffats' new house was different from the yellow house.

   The new house was smaller with a huge front yard and a small backyard. It had few trees and only one arbor. However, they knew that eventually there might be many things they would like.

Vocabulary Crossword

Across:

2. supplies
5. threateningly
7. extended
11. comfort
12. aggressively
17. leisurely strolled
18. in full agreement
19. dislike; disapproval
20. passionately; zealously

Down:

1. inconvenient
3. bridge
4. quiet; restrained
6. to mimic
8. scornful
9. enemies; competitors
10. unconcerned
13. moving uncontrollably
14. shocked
15. thoughtful
16. urgently begged

Word Bank

adversaries	indifferent
aghast	inopportune
belligerently	menacingly
careening	pensive
consolation	protruded
contempt	provisions
disdainful	sauntered
fervently	subdued
impersonate	unanimous
implored	viaduct

Personification

Circle the noun that is being personified. Underline the words that show human characteristics.

Personification: to give human characteristics to a thing or idea.

Example: The water defied the cold.

1. But the wind was now on their backs and urged them up the street swiftly.
2. In her imagination Jane's feet carefully followed each step of the dance with graceful ease.
3. The wind tried to snatch their hats from their heads.
4. Madame was on the porch wearing a rather disapproving air.
5. The rooms were empty, but they wore a look of expectancy.
6. The thunder cracked its mighty whip across the sky as the lightning sped through the air.
7. The engine of the Bay State Express was just itching to be off.
8. The freighters in the train yard beckoned to him invitingly until he could resist no longer.
9. The longer she stared at it the louder the sign screamed that this was no longer her house.
10. The leaves fairly danced across the page of Jane's autumn drawing.

Character, Setting, Plot

Write a short phrase or sentence to answer each question.

1. What does the term "character" mean? The characters are the main people in the story. They are who the story is about.
2. Name the members of the Moffat family. Who is the oldest child? Who is the youngest? The Moffat family consists of Mama, Sylvie, Joe, Jane, and Rufus. Sylvie is the oldest child and Rufus is the youngest.
3. What does the term "setting" mean? The setting tells the time and place in which the story takes place.
4. What is the setting of *The Moffats*? In what region of the country is the imaginary town of Cranbury located? The setting of the Moffats is in the early 1900s. It takes place in the New England area of the U.S., specifically in Connecticut.
5. What does the term "plot" mean? The plot is the action of the story, or what actually takes place in the story.

Multiple Choice

Circle the letter that BEST answers each question.

1. How did the Murdocks become involved with the Moffats?

   a. Their daughter, Letitia, was a good friend of Jane's.

   b. Mrs. Murdock asked Mama to sew a dress for her.

   (c.) They noticed the yellow house while Jane was cleaning mud off of the "For Sale" sign.

   d. Mr. Murdock inspected the Moffats' roof for leaks.

2. What was Mama's reaction to the news that Joe and Jane had lost the money?

   (a.) She was calm and understanding. She tried to make the best of it.

   b. She thought of ways for Joe to earn money to make up for what he had lost.

   c. She was irate and sent them to bed with no supper.

   d. She stared at them in disbelief.

3. How did the Moffats justify their Sunday adventure as a good deed?

   a. They reasoned that the Salvation Army was just like Sunday school.

   b. They saw that the man was tired and that they could let him rest.

   c. They thought that helping the man was better than being late for Sunday school.

   (d.) all of the above

4. How did meeting Mr. Pennypepper affect Jane's day?

   a. Jane was worried he would tell her to go to school.

   b. Jane was happy to meet someone new and invited him to meet her family.

   (c.) Jane was afraid she would be arrested because she mimicked his interesting walk.

   d. Jane was disappointed because he wanted to sell her house.

5. What was Mama's occupation?

   a. She was a dance teacher.

   b. She was an art teacher.

   c. She was a house cleaner.

   (d.) She was a dressmaker. (a seamstress)

6. Why did Rufus want to ride the Second Avenue trolley?

a. He was tired and did not want to walk to the beach.

b. He had never ridden a trolley before.

c. He wanted to see if he could ride the trolley for free.

(d.) He wanted to learn about becoming a motorman.

7. How did Jane break the Moffats' sharing code?

a. She bought caramels for each of her siblings.

b. She saved her nickel instead of spending it on something for her siblings.

(c.) She spent her nickel on an ice cream cone for herself.

d. She gave her nickel to Mr. Brooney's daughter.

8. What was the second sign on the yellow house? Why was it there?

a. Free Kittens; Catherine had new kittens.

(b.) Quarantine; Rufus had scarlet fever.

c. Vote for Dr. Witty; Dr. Witty was running for mayor of Cranbury.

d. New Lower Price; The yellow house had not been sold yet.

9. What was the positive outcome of the boys' train adventure?

(a.) The experience on the train made Hughie want to go to school so he could become an engineer.

b. There was a kind man who helped the boys return home.

c. They returned home so late that they did not have to return to school.

d. The teacher never noticed that they were missing.

10. Who was Madame, and what purpose did she serve?

a. She was Mama's boss and told Mama what to do.

(b.) She was a dressmaker's dummy and could mimic anyone's body.

c. She was an assistant to the chief of police who told him to look for Jane.

d. She was the Moffats' pet cat.

Short Answer

Answer the following questions in complete sentences.

1. List two differences in activities and surroundings that you have noticed between the Moffats' life and your own. Rufus plays marbles, an airplane flying overhead is an unusual event, Jane knits, they have a potbellied stove, Mama makes dresses for a living, the For Sale sign is nailed directly to the house, the hitching post, trolleys were a common way to travel.

2. How did Sylvie, Jane, and Joe each feel about dancing lessons?
Sylvie loved her dance lessons and had a natural talent for it.
Jane liked to imagine herself as a graceful dancer, but actually wasn't a good dancer.
Joe disliked lessons very much, wasn't any good at dancing, and tried to avoid the lessons.

3. Describe two ways the Moffats tried to save money. Jane put cardboard inside her shoe where the sole had worn away. Joe sifted through the ashes to find lumps of coal they could reburn. Mama was managing the money very carefully, and she told Joe to count the change carefully.

4. Give one example of Jane's overactive imagination. Possible answers: While in the bread box she pictured herself as a princess locked in a cavern; Jane was frightened by the ghost she had helped to build; she imagined herself to be a graceful dancer; she imagined she was the little match girl; she imagined the horse had wings, was the wooden horse of Troy, and was a bridge.

5. Describe how the Moffats' new house was different from the yellow house.
The new house was smaller with a huge front yard and a small backyard. It had few trees and only one arbor. However, they knew that eventually there might be many things they would like.

Paragraph

Write a paragraph (at least five sentences) about your favorite character in *The Moffats*. Include an introductory sentence and a concluding sentence. Explain why you like this character best.

Appendix

Eleanor Estes, 1906-1988

Eleanor Estes was born in 1906, as Eleanor Ruth Rosenfield. She was the third of four children, and like the mother of her Moffat characters, her mother was a widowed dressmaker. She was born in the town of West Haven, Connecticut, and grew up in New Haven, where she later worked as a children's librarian.

Estes' writing career began after she suffered a case of tuberculosis. While still bedridden during her recovery, Estes began writing down some of her childhood memories. These memories were later turned into full-length children's books. Her first novel was *The Moffats*, written in 1941. In this book, set in the safe, serene town of Cranbury, we see her own hometown of New Haven, and experience delightful portions of her own childhood through the character of Jane Moffat.

Estes had a gift for portraying unique characters in a manner that allows the reader to understand and see life through the eyes and feelings of a child. In her books, family life is experienced as warm and full of affection, sometimes sobering, and often humorous. Her novel *Ginger Pye* won the Newbery Medal, and three of her other books were Newbery Honor award winners. By the time of her death in 1988, she had written nineteen children's books and one adult novel.

More books by Eleanor Estes:

The Middle Moffat
Rufus M.
The Moffat Museum

Ginger Pye
Pinky Pye

The Witch Family
The Hundred Dresses
Miranda the Great

1889	Electric light is installed in the White House
1900	*The Wonderful Wizard of Oz* published by L. Frank Baum
1903	Ice cream cones become popular
	First World Series baseball game played (Boston vs. Pittsburg)
	First flight of Orville & Wilbur Wright's airplane at Kitty Hawk, NC
1905	About this time, electricity is becoming more common in homes, replacing gas
1908	William Howard Taft elected president (1909-1913)
	Boy Scouts of America founded
	Henry Ford introduces his Model T; first mass-produced, affordable car
1910	Earth passes through the tail of Halley's Comet
	Girl Scouts of America founded
1912	The *Titanic* sinks
1913	Woodrow Wilson elected president (1913-1921)
1914	WWI begins in Europe (U.S. enters war in 1917)
	War ends in 1919
1916	Norman Rockwell paints his first "Saturday Evening Post" cover

The Economy / Recessions

Panic of 1907 — Run on banks, the stock exchange fell 50%
This led to the creation of a federal reserve system.

Panic of 1910-1911

Fun Facts to Know

Popular books: *The Secret Garden*, *Tarzan of the Apes*

Popular toys: erector sets, tinker toys, Lincoln Logs

Bicycles, first invented in the early 1800s, were gaining in popularity and use in the 1900s, especially by women. Bicycles even played an important role in female emancipation.

Cost of Common Goods

newspaper	$ .25
McMillan Latin book	$ .40
loaf of bread	$ .05
gallon of milk	$ .34
1 pound of sugar	$ .05

Does this time period in American history interest you?
Below are some books about boys and girls, set in the early 1900s.

**What Katy Did*, by Susan Coolidge

(First published in 1872 and currently out of print, but you should be able to find it in a good library.) Following the death of her mother, Katy, the eldest of her siblings, must learn to be brave and take care of her family after an unexpected accident.

**Understood Betsy*, by Dorothy Canfield Fisher

Elizabeth Ann is sent to live with her horrible cousins in Vermont. Formerly sickly and somewhat spoiled, she now has to adapt to an entirely different type of life. A humorous, affectionate story of life in the country.

**The Call of the Wild*
**White Fang*, both by Jack London

Exciting books about men and dogs that take place in the Alaskan wilderness.

**I Am Lavina Cumming*, by Susan Lowell

The story of a girl living with her mother, father, and brothers on a ranch in Arizona territory. After the loss of her mother, Lavina's father sends her to live with an aunt in Santa Cruz. Here she must adjust to city life and lives through the San Francisco earthquake.

**Roller Skates*, by Ruth Sawyer

Lucinda Wyman is ten and lives in New York City in the 1890s. She stays with a teacher for a year, where she is free to rollerskate to school, make friends with various kinds of people, and have many adventures.

**Goodbye to the Trees,* by Vicky Shiefman

Fagel Fratrizsky must leave her family in Russia and travel by ship to live in Boston. She lives with relatives, works as a dressmaker, has adventures, and worries if she will ever find a way for her family to join her in America.

**Dragonwings*, by Lawrence Yep

Moon Shadow Lee works with his father in San Francisco in 1903. But he and his father really love to make kites and flying machines. They even receive advice from the Wright brothers!

Map of New Dollar Street

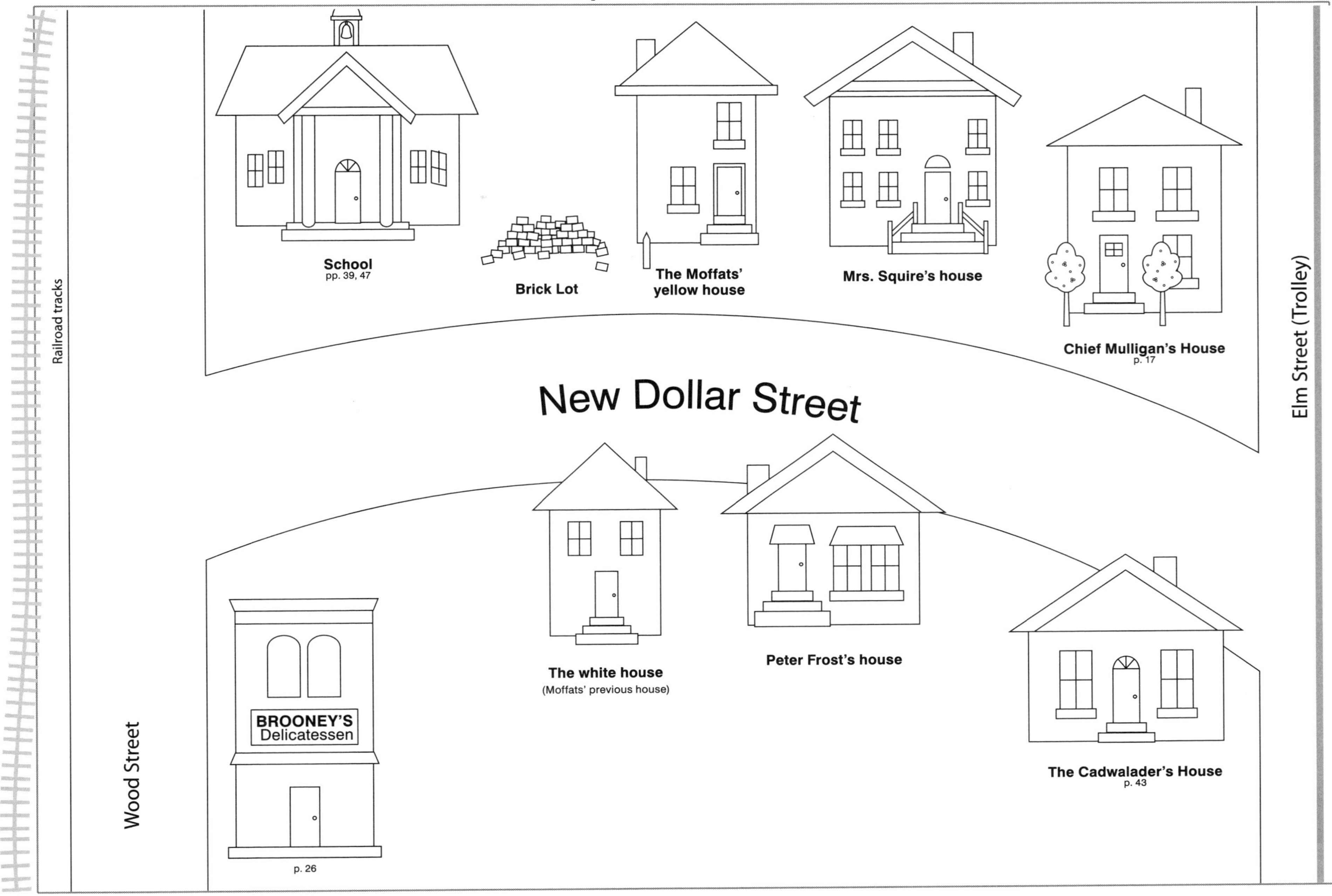

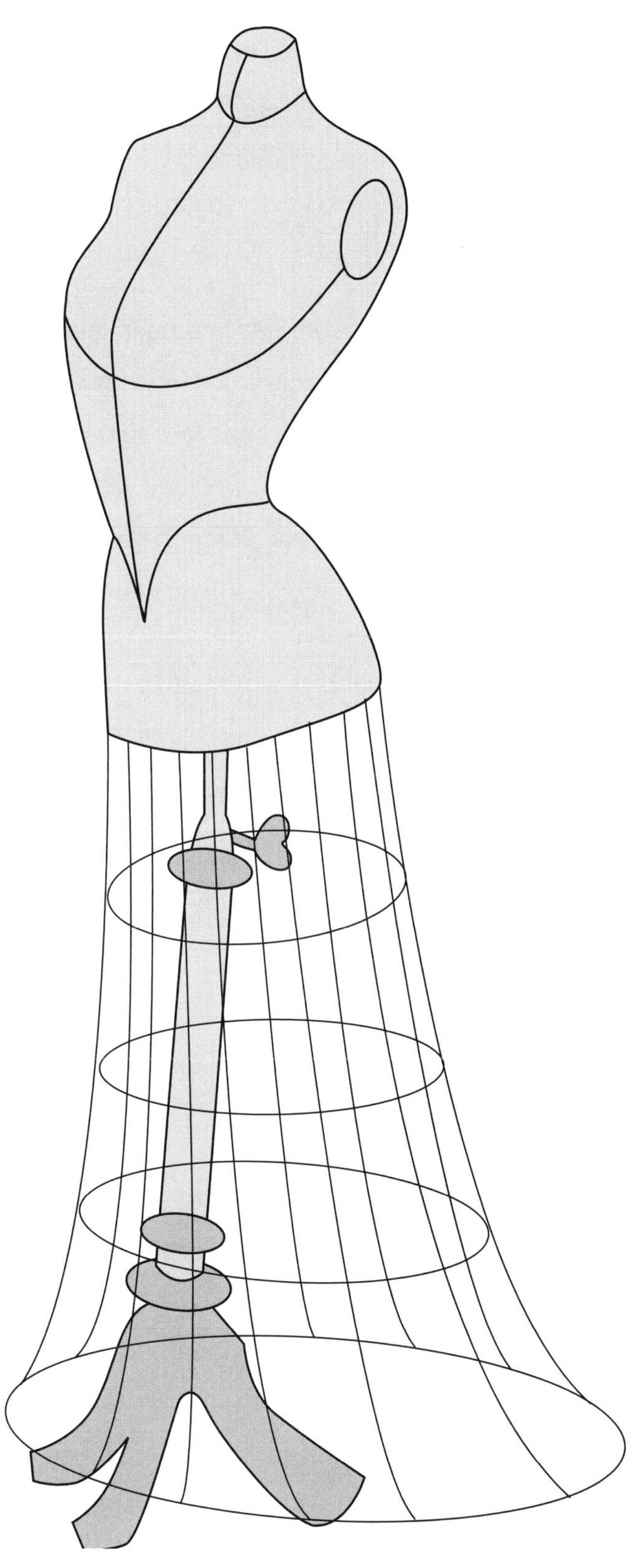

The Little Match Girl

(as referenced in Chapter 7: Another Sign on the Yellow House)

Most terribly cold it was; it snowed, and was nearly quite dark, and evening—the last evening of the year. In this cold and darkness there went along the street a poor little girl, bareheaded, and with naked feet. When she left home she had slippers on, it is true; but what was the good of that? They were very large slippers, which her mother had hitherto worn; so large were they; and the poor little thing lost them as she scuffled away across the street, because of two carriages that rolled by dreadfully fast.

One slipper was nowhere to be found; the other had been laid hold of by an urchin, and off he ran with it; he thought it would do capitally for a cradle when he some day or other should have children himself. So the little maiden walked on with her tiny naked feet, that were quite red and blue from cold. She carried a quantity of matches in an old apron, and she held a bundle of them in her hand. Nobody had bought anything of her the whole livelong day; no one had given her a single farthing.

She crept along trembling with cold and hunger—a very picture of sorrow, the poor little thing!

The flakes of snow covered her long fair hair, which fell in beautiful curls around her neck; but of that, of course, she never once now thought. From all the windows the candles were gleaming, and it smelt so deliciously of roast goose, for you know it was New Year's Eve; yes, of that she thought.

In a corner formed by two houses, of which one advanced more than the other, she seated herself down and cowered together. Her little feet she had drawn close up to her, but she grew colder and colder, and to go home she did not venture, for she had not sold any matches and could not bring a farthing of money: from her father she would certainly get blows, and at home it was cold too, for above her she had only the roof, through which the wind whistled, even though the largest cracks were stopped up with straw and rags.

Her little hands were almost numbed with cold. Oh! a match might afford her a world of comfort, if she only dared take a single one out of the bundle, draw it against the wall, and warm her fingers by it. She drew one out. "Rischt!" how it blazed, how it burnt! It was a warm, bright flame, like a candle, as she held her hands over it: it was a wonderful light. It seemed really to the little maiden as though she were sitting before a large iron stove, with burnished brass feet and a brass ornament at top. The fire burned with such blessed influence; it warmed so delightfully. The little girl had already stretched out her feet to warm them too; but—the small flame went out, the stove vanished: she had only the remains of the burnt-out match in her hand.

She rubbed another against the wall: it burned brightly, and where the light fell on the wall, there the wall became transparent like a veil, so that she could see into the room. On the table was spread a snow-white tablecloth; upon it was a splendid porcelain service, and the roast goose was steaming famously with its stuffing of apple and dried plums. And what was still more capital to behold was, the goose hopped down from the dish, reeled about on the floor with knife and fork in its breast, till it came up to the poor little girl; when—the match went out and nothing but the thick, cold, damp wall was left behind. She lighted another match. Now there she was sitting under the most magnificent Christmas tree: it was still larger, and more decorated, than the one which she had seen through the glass door in the rich merchant's house.

Thousands of lights were burning on the green branches, and gaily colored pictures, such as she had seen in the shop windows, looked down upon her. The little maiden stretched out her hands towards them when—the match went out. The lights of the Christmas tree rose higher and higher, she saw them now as stars in heaven; one fell down and formed a long trail of fire.

"Someone is just dead!" said the little girl; for her old grandmother, the only person who had loved her, and who was now no more, had told her that when a star falls, a soul ascends to God. She drew another match against the wall: it was again light, and in the lustre there stood the old grandmother, so bright and radiant, so mild, and with such an expression of love.

"Grandmother!" cried the little one. "Oh, take me with you! You go away when the match burns out; you vanish like the warm stove, like the delicious roast goose, and like the magnificent Christmas tree!" And she rubbed the whole bundle of matches quickly against the wall, for she wanted to be quite sure of keeping her grandmother near her. And the matches gave such a brilliant light that it was brighter than at noon-day: never formerly had the grandmother been so beautiful and so tall. She took the little maiden on her arm, and both flew in brightness and in joy so high, so very high, and then above was neither cold, nor hunger, nor anxiety—they were with God.

But in the corner, at the cold hour of dawn, sat the poor girl, with rosy cheeks and with a smiling mouth, leaning against the wall—frozen to death on the last evening of the old year. Stiff and stark sat the child there with her matches, of which one bundle had been burnt. "She wanted to warm herself," people said. No one had the slightest suspicion of what beautiful things she had seen; no one even dreamed of the splendor in which, with her grandmother, she had entered on the joys of a new year.

Daisy Bell

Melody and text by Harry Dacre, 1892

(as referenced in Chapter 7: Another Sign on the Yellow House)

There is a flower within my heart,
Daisy, Daisy!
Planted one day by a glancing dart,
Planted by Daisy Bell!
Whether she loves me or loves me not,
Sometimes it's hard to tell;
Yet I am longing to share the lot
Of beautiful Daisy Bell!

Chorus:
Daisy Daisy,
Give me your answer do!
I'm half crazy,
All for the love of you!
It won't be a stylish marriage,
I can't afford a carriage,
But you'll look sweet upon the seat
Of a bicycle built for two!

We will go "tandem" as man and wife,
Daisy, Daisy!
Ped'ling away down the road of life,
I and my Daisy Bell!
When the road's dark we can despise
P'liceman and lamps as well;
There are bright lights in the dazzling eyes
Of beautiful Daisy Bell!

Chorus

I will stand by you in "wheel" or woe,
Daisy, Daisy!
You'll be the bell(e) which I'll ring, you know!
Sweet little Daisy Bell!
You'll take the lead in each trip we take,
Then if I don't do well;
I will permit you to use the brake,
My beautiful Daisy Bell!!!

Chorus

The Wind

by Robert Louis Stevenson

(quoted in part by Jane in Chapter 12)

I saw you toss the kites on high
And blow the birds about the sky;
And all around I heard you pass,
Like ladies' skirts across the grass—
    O wind, a-blowing all day long,
    O wind, that sings so loud a song!

I saw the different things you did,
But always you yourself you hid.
I felt you push, I heard you call,
I could not see yourself at all—
    O wind, a-blowing all day long,
    O wind, that sings so loud a song!

O you that are so strong and cold,
O blower, are you young or old?
Are you a beast of field and tree,
Or just a stronger child than me?
    O wind, a-blowing all day long,
    O wind, that sings so loud a song!

Our House

by Dorothy Brown Thompson

Our house is small—
The lawn and all
Can scarcely hold the flowers,
Yet every bit,
The whole of it,
Is precious, for it's ours!

From door to door,
From roof to floor,
From wall to wall we love it;
We wouldn't change
For something strange
One shabby corner of it!

The space complete
In cubic feet
From cellar floor to rafter
Just measures right,
And not too tight,
For us, and friends, and laughter!

Discussion Questions
Answer Key

Discussion questions that have a * are NECESSARY to discuss with students as they may appear on a test and are generally important in understanding the full flavor of the story.

Chapter 1, Part 1: The Yellow House on New Dollar Street

1. From your observations so far in the story, describe the main character, Jane.

   Jane is a typical, happy little nine-year-old girl. She finds some tasks difficult to do and admires the way her mother does them with ease. She enjoys playing outdoors and with her doll. She has a unique personality, is somewhat "spunky," and has a definite opinion about the world around her.

Chapter 1, Part 2: The Yellow House on New Dollar Street

1. *What differences in daily activities and surroundings do you notice between the Moffats' life and your own?

   Some possible differences could include Rufus playing marbles, an airplane flying overhead is an unusual event, Jane knits, they have a potbellied stove, Mama makes dresses for a living, the For Sale sign is nailed directly to the front of the house, there is a hitching post, and trolleys were a regular way of travel.

Chapter 2, Part 1: Jane and the Chief of Police

1. Using the descriptions from this chapter, add Chief Mulligan's house and Mr. Brooney's delicatessen to the map that you drew in the last chapter.

   No answer necessary.

Chapter 2, Part 2: Jane and the Chief of Police

1. Jane had convinced herself that she could be arrested for irritating the Chief of Police. What do you think Mama would have said if Jane had told her about these fears? After she confessed her fears to him, how did the Chief's reaction change Jane's view of him?

   Answers will vary: Mama may have laughed like Chief Mulligan did; she would no doubt have quieted Jane's fears and assured her that while mimicking someone is not polite, it is not a crime. When Jane saw he was not angry and was laughing at her error, she began to see him as a real person instead of only as an authority figure. She saw that he was kind, had a good sense of humor, and treated her with respect.

2. Describe the event that led to Jane's discovery in the bread box.

   Mr. Brooney and the baker had a disagreement about the number of loaves of bread that had been delivered that morning, so they opened the box to be sure none of the loaves had been overlooked and left inside. There they found Jane, hiding.

Chapter 3, Part 1: The First Day of School

1. Why did Rufus disobey his mother to follow Hughie? Did Rufus make a wise decision? How else might he have handled the situation?

   Mrs. Moffat told the children never to go onto the railroad tracks, but Mr. Pennypepper told Rufus to make sure Hughie stayed at school. His decision was not wise. He should have asked his teacher for help. Other answers will vary.

2. Add the school and Nelly Cadwalader's house to your map.

   The location of the school is described on pp. 39 and 47. The location of the Cadwalader's house is described on p. 43.

Chapter 3, Part 2: The First Day of School

1. Find the New York, New Haven, Hartford, Boston train route on a map. Where do you think the imaginary town of Cranbury might be located? You will need a map of the New York, Connecticut, and Massachusetts coastline. (Note p. 51, paragraph beginning, "The two boys looked back …")

   Cranbury might be on the East Coast, near the towns of New Haven and Hartford, CT.

Chapter 4, Part 1: A Horse and Wagon

1. How did Rufus learn sections of the catechism, Latin, and history? Have you ever learned something in a similar manner?

   Rufus learned these things from hearing his older siblings recite them aloud many times.

2. Research more information about the Salvation Army. Have its activities changed over the years?

   Answers will vary.

Chapter 4, Part 2: A Horse and Wagon

1. Discuss the imagery of the quote above. How do the words the author chose give you a vivid picture of the storm?

   Imagery includes, "the heavens opened," "the wind tore branches," "thunder cracked like a whip," and "lightning sizzled."

Chapter 5, Part 1: The Ghost in the Attic

1. Explain the difference between Miss Partridge and Mr. Allgood. Which teacher did the students prefer? Why?

   The students looked forward to Miss Partridge because their time with her was always pleasant and they had fewer restrictions when they were with her. She smiled all the time and was very encouraging. The students feared Mr. Allgood, who was very strict and found fault with everything the students did.

Chapter 5, Part 2: The Ghost in the Attic

1. What happened in the attic to scare Peter Frost? In what ways did the Moffats frighten themselves as much as they frightened Peter?

   Joe flashed the flashlight on and off, displaying the stuffed animals. Madame-the-ghost began rolling toward them, dragging heavy chains. Jane yelled Peter's name in a shrill voice. Several other things happened that weren't part of their plan but added to the feeling of fright (i.e., Catherine-the-cat dragging Madame wildly around the attic while howling, the wind and the banging shutters, Joe's flashlight went out, and Rufus and Jane howling with fright).

2. Read the English fairy tale "Jack and the Beanstalk." Why do you think the events in the attic made Rufus think of this story?

   Rufus was feeling the suspense and fear of the moment and comparing it to the same feeling he got when hearing the story of "Jack and the Beanstalk."

Chapter 6, Part 1: The Sailor's Hornpipe

1. In what way is the special arrangement of the Moffats' dancing lessons related to the setting of the story?

   The setting is during the early 1900s when "times are hard." The book tells us Mama could not afford to give her children the luxury of dance lessons without the special arrangement of trading lessons for sewing.

2. The author tells us that Joe hated parties and dancing and found every way he could to avoid learning, even while in dance class. What evidence do you see in this chapter that, despite his disinterest, Joe is still actually learning how to dance?

   Despite his efforts to hide and avoid participating during dance lessons, Joe is still able to flawlessly dance the sailor's hornpipe with Sugar once he forgets that everyone is watching him. His dislike of dancing may be connected with his fear of failing at it.

Chapter 6, Part 2: The Sailor's Hornpipe

1. Why did Joe begin to enjoy the dance partway through his performance?

   Joe was able to remember the steps when he realized the dog was looking to him for cues. As he sensed that people were no longer looking at him, but at the dog, he relaxed and the dancing became fun.

2. Why did Joe leave the performance whistling, even though he did not get the promised ten cents?

   Miss Chichester had praised him, saying he was the best in the program. The feeling of success was a better reward than money.

3. Have you ever had to perform for an audience when you felt unprepared? How did you feel?

   Answers will vary.

Chapter 7, Part 1: Another Sign on the Yellow House

1. Read Hans Christian Andersen's fairy tale, *The Little Match Girl.* Explain why Jane identified with this story. (One version of this story can be found in the Appendix.)

   Jane identified with *The Little Match Girl* because she was alone and scared. When she saw the cold lamplighter outside the window, it reminded her of the story, and she pictured herself poor, cold, and huddled in a doorway, "lighting her last match with her poor, frozen fingers …"

Chapter 7, Part 2: Another Sign on the Yellow House

1. *List some specific differences between how illness was treated in the Moffats' time compared to today's methods.

   Some specific differences would be that the Moffats were quarantined in the house, the doctor visited Rufus in their home rather than at his office, and a grocery boy came to their house to deliver groceries.

2. Look in the Appendix for the song "Daisy Bell." What is another name for a bicycle-built-for-two?

   Another name for a bicycle-built-for-two is a "tandem" bicycle.

3. What other fictitious or real people do you know that were affected by scarlet fever?

   Other fictitious or real people who suffered from scarlet fever include Beth in *Little Women,* the boy in *The Velveteen Rabbit*, Mary Ingalls in the *Little House* series, and possibly Helen Keller.

Chapter 8, Part 1: The Coal Barge

1. Why did the Moffats need coal? What is a coal barge?

   The Moffats needed the coal because they burned coal as their only source of heat to stay warm in the winter. A coal barge is a boat on which coal is shipped from the mine to the port of a city.

Chapter 8, Part 2: The Coal Barge

1. List some advantages to the Moffats' simpler lifestyle.

   Some advantages to the Moffats' simpler lifestyle include the fact that they had to work hard to live. This helped to develop a strong character and a tight family unit that worked together for their common good. Other advantages were they weren't wasteful; they used things up, mended clothing, and made do with what they had. In general, things cost less money. Doctors visited your home, making it easier on the person who was ill. Groceries were also delivered to the door, when necessary, saving time and energy for the buyer.

Chapter 9, Part 1: Share and Share Alike

1. *List examples from the book of Jane's overactive imagination.

   Examples of Jane's overactive imagination: Ch. 2 - While in the bread box she pictured herself as a princess locked in a cavern. Ch. 5 - Jane was frightened by the ghost she had helped to build. Ch. 6 - She imagined herself to be a graceful dancer. Ch. 7 - She imagined she was the little match girl. Ch. 9 - She imagined the horse had wings, was the wooden horse of Troy, and was a bridge.

Chapter 9, Part 2: Share and Share Alike

1. What were some of the other things Jane could have bought with her nickel? What can a nickel buy now?

   Jane could have bought 20 caramels, 10 sticks of licorice, 10 peppermint patties, or 4 sheets of paper dolls. Now a nickel might buy a used item at a garage sale or perhaps a single piece of candy at a candy store.

Chapter 10, Part 1: Mud and Murdocks

1. A family sometimes has to move from a house that is familiar and dear to them. Why would that be difficult? How might it affect various members of the family?

   It might be difficult moving from a house because you have lived there a long time and everything is familiar to you. You may have made good friends and neighbors. You may be moving farther away from relatives you love. Change can be frightening, and a move brings many changes. Sometimes a family is not able to bring their pets along to the new location. Moving also takes lots of energy and work; it is physically tiring. It may affect members of the family differently. Parents may be more excited because they are looking forward to a better house, a better job, or some other better situation. But parents will also bear the brunt of the work in moving. Children may miss their friends, or have to change schools, with unfamiliar students, teachers, and buildings. Older children may have to leave a good job behind and start over in a strange city.

Chapter 10, Part 2: Mud and Murdocks

1. Research Harry Houdini. When did he live? What were some of his famous escapist acts?

   Answers may vary, depending on the research.

Chapter 11, Part 1: The New Second Avenue Trolley Line

1. Why did the children pick out the tinfoil from the empty cigarette cases and gum wrappers?

   During the early 1900s, people strived to conserve and reuse materials. The children were collecting the foil in order to recycle it.

2. When Rufus boarded the trolley, the driver assumed he was not yet six years old and said he did not need to pay. What was Rufus' response to this surprise? Was it the best response? Why or why not?

   Rufus pocketed his nickel without mentioning that he was six. Answers will vary, but he should have told the truth.

Chapter 11, Part 2: The New Second Avenue Trolley Line

1. How would you describe each of the two trolley motormen? Use plenty of descriptive detail.

   The first motorman was an old man with a walrus mustache. He wore his hat straight over his eyes and took the business of driving his trolley very seriously. He had a rather sour temperament. The other driver was an impudent young man. He wore his hat tipped on the back of his head and sat slouched on his stool. He spoke insultingly to the older man.

Chapter 12, Part 1: The Last Chapter in the Yellow House

1. What did each of the Moffat children do "one last time" on the last day in the yellow house? Why do you think they felt they needed to do these things?

   Joe climbed the old apple tree. Rufus shinned up the cherry tree. Sylvie made last minute entries in her diary. Jane did not have anything definite to do and was glad when Mama sent her to the movers. Answers will vary.

2. How did Jane look at the new house? When has she done this before? What was she looking at then? Why does she like to look at things this way?

   She looked at the new house the upside-down way, from between her legs. She did the same thing in the first chapter of the book when she was looking at New Dollar Street. In that chapter the book tells us she thinks it makes everything look cleaner and brighter.

Chapter 12, Part 2: The Last Chapter in the Yellow House

1. The end of something is often memorable and can create emotional responses. Can you think of a "last chapter" in your life? How did you feel? What did you learn from the experience?

   Answers will vary.

2. In this chapter Jane recited lines from R. L. Stevenson's poem "The Wind." Read the poem in the Appendix and memorize it.

Quizzes & Final Test

(reproducible for classroom use)

The Moffats Quiz I
Chapters 1-6

Name ______________________

Date ______________________

Write the letter of the vocabulary word on the line in front of its definition.

1. _______	to mimic	a.	viaduct
2. _______	aggressively	b.	subdued
3. _______	leisurely strolled	c.	impersonate
4. _______	in full agreement	d.	pensive
5. _______	supplies	e.	sauntered
6. _______	moving uncontrollably	f.	belligerently
7. _______	thoughtful	g.	contempt
8. _______	bridge	h.	unanimous
9. _______	dislike; disapproval	i.	provisions
10. _______	quiet; restrained	j.	careening

Match each name below with the character description.

Jane	**Capt. Salvation Army**	**Hughie Pudge**	**Mr. Allgood**	**Mr. Pennypepper**
Peter Frost	**Miss Chichester**	**Mama**	**Madame**	**Chief Mulligan**

1. ______________________ told Joe his impromptu performance made a success of the recital
2. ______________________ works as a seamstress for a living
3. ______________________ causes the children to sit as straight as ramrods
4. ______________________ likes to look at things the upside-down way
5. ______________________ could only be awakened by the beat of a drum
6. ______________________ used as a model for Mama's customers
7. ______________________ decided to become an engineer when he grows up.
8. ______________________ laughed so hard that tears ran into his whiskers
9. ______________________ an insufferable bully
10. ______________________ nods politely to everyone he passes

Choose the **best** answer for each question.

1. What is Mama's occupation?
   a. a dressmaker
   b. a dance teacher
   c. an art teacher
   d. a house cleaner

2. Who is Madame, and what purpose does she serve?
   a. She is Mama's boss and tells Mama what to do.
   b. She is a dressmaker's dummy and can mimic anyone's body.
   c. She is an assistant to the chief of police who tells him to look for Jane.
   d. She is the Moffats' pet cat.

3. How does meeting Mr. Pennypepper affect Jane's day?
   a. Jane is worried he will tell her to go to school.
   b. Jane is afraid she will be arrested because she mimics his interesting walk.
   c. Jane is happy to meet someone new and invites him to meet her family.
   d. Jane is disappointed because he wants to sell her house.

4. What was the positive outcome of the boys' train adventure?
   a. There was a kind man who helped the boys return home.
   b. They returned home so late that they did not have to return to school.
   c. The experience on the train makes Hughie want to go to school so he can become an engineer.
   d. The teacher never noticed that they were missing.

5. How do the Moffats justify their Sunday adventure as a good deed?
   a. They reason that the Salvation Army is just like Sunday school.
   b. They see that the man is tired and that they can let him rest.
   c. They think that helping the man is better than being late for Sunday school.
   d. all of the above

Answer the following questions in complete sentences.

1. List two differences in activities and surroundings that you have noticed between the Moffats' life and your own. ______________________________

2. How do Mr. Pennypepper's instructions conflict with Mama's instructions? ______________________________

3. List two grudges the Moffats had against Peter Frost. ______________________________

4. Who lived in the yellow house before the Moffats? What was his occupation? ______________________________

5. How do Sylvie, Jane, and Joe each feel about dancing lessons?

   Sylvie: ______________________________

   Jane: ______________________________

   Joe: ______________________________

The Moffats Quiz 2
Chapters 7-12

Name ______________________________

Date ______________________________

Write the letter of the vocabulary word on the line in front of its definition.

1. _______	enemies; competitors	a.	protruded
2. _______	comfort	b.	inopportune
3. _______	unconcerned; uninterested	c.	aghast
4. _______	passionately; zealously	d.	consolation
5. _______	shocked; dismayed	e.	indifferent
6. _______	threateningly	f.	implored
7. _______	scornful	g.	fervently
8. _______	urgently begged	h.	disdainful
9. _______	extended	i.	adversaries
10. _______	inconvenient	j.	menacingly

Match each name below with the character description.

Joe	**motorman McCann**	**Sylvie**	**Letitia Murdock**	**motorman O'Brien**
Boots	**Tilly Cadwalader**	**Jane**	**Rufus**	**Dr. Belknap**

1. ______________________________ spends the first week of summer vacation at Camp Lincoln
2. ______________________________ a good, jolly man who diagnoses Rufus' scarlet fever
3. ______________________________ practices his stilt-walking in the backyard
4. ______________________________ the only girl in her family that wears her hair high on her head
5. ______________________________ wanted to ride the trolley to see the business about the red lights
6. ______________________________ shows marks of personality that lift her above the usual run of cats and kittens
7. ______________________________ was a pig, that's what, a pig
8. ______________________________ would ring the doorbell, then run to the back door and knock
9. ______________________________ wears his hat tipped on his head and sits all slouchy on his stool
10. ______________________________ an old man who takes driving a trolley car very seriously

1. What is the second sign on the yellow house? Why is it there?
   a. Free Kittens!; Catherine had new kittens.
   b. Quarantine; Rufus has scarlet fever.
   c. New Lower Price; The yellow house has not been sold yet.
   d. Vote for Dr. Witty; Dr. Witty is running for mayor of Cranbury.

2. What is Mama's reaction to the news that Joe and Jane have lost the money to buy coal?
   a. She is irate and sends them to bed with no supper.
   b. She is calm and understanding. She tries to make the best of it.
   c. She thinks of ways for Joe to earn money to make up for what he has lost.
   d. She stares at them in disbelief.

3. How does Jane break the Moffat's sharing code?
   a. She buys caramels for each of her siblings.
   b. She saves her nickel instead of spending it on something for her siblings.
   c. She spends her nickel on an ice cream cone for herself.
   d. She gives her nickel to Mr. Brooney's daughter.

4. How do the Murdocks become involved with the Moffats?
   a. Their daughter, Letitia, is a good friend of Jane's.
   b. They notice the yellow house while Jane is cleaning mud off of the For Sale sign.
   c. Mrs. Murdock asks Mama to sew a dress for her.
   d. Mr. Murdock inspects the Moffats' roof for leaks.

5. Why does Rufus want to ride the Second Avenue trolley?
   a. He is tired and does not want to walk to the beach.
   b. He has never ridden a trolley before.
   c. He wants to see if he can ride the trolley for free.
   d. He wants to learn about becoming a motorman.

Answer the following questions in complete sentences.

1. Give one example of how illness is treated differently in the Moffats' time compared to today's methods. ______________________________

2. Describe two ways the Moffats try to save money. ______________________________

3. Describe an example of Jane's overactive imagination. Give details. ______________________________

4. What excitement is encountered on the trolley? ______________________________

5. Describe how the Moffats' new house is different from the yellow house. ______________________________

The Moffats Final Test

Name ______________________

Date ______________________

Vocabulary: Write the letter of the vocabulary word next to its definition.

1. _______ supplies
2. _______ to mimic
3. _______ dislike; disapproval
4. _______ in full agreement
5. _______ thoughtful
6. _______ aggressively
7. _______ scornful
8. _______ enemies; competitors
9. _______ urgently begged
10. _______ unconcerned; uninterested

a. disdainful
b. impersonate
c. implored
d. unanimous
e. adversaries
f. pensive
g. provisions
h. indifferent
i. belligerently
j. contempt

Character Identification: Choose the name that matches each description and write it on the line.

Mr. Allgood	**Letitia Murdock**	**Jane**	**Peter Frost**	**Chief Mulligan**
Rufus	**Miss Chichester**	**Joe**	**Mama**	**Boots**

1. ______________________ told Joe his impromptu performance made a success of the recital
2. ______________________ causes the children to sit as straight as ramrods
3. ______________________ likes to look at things the upside-down way
4. ______________________ laughed so hard that tears ran into his whiskers
5. ______________________ an insufferable bully
6. ______________________ practices his stilt walking in the backyard
7. ______________________ wanted to ride the trolley to see the business about the red lights
8. ______________________ shows marks of personality that lift her above the usual run of cats and kittens
9. ______________________ would ring and ring the doorbell, then run around to the back door and knock
10. ______________________ works as a seamstress for a living

Personification: Circle the noun that is being personified. Underline the words that show human characteristics.

1. The freighters in the train yard beckoned to him invitingly until he could resist no longer.
2. But the wind was now on their backs and urged them up the street swiftly.
3. The wind tried to snatch their hats from their heads.
4. Madame was on the porch wearing a rather disapproving air.
5. The engine of the Bay State Express was just itching to be off.
6. The longer she stared at it the louder the sign screamed that this was no longer her house.
7. In her imagination Jane's feet carefully followed each step of the dance with graceful ease.
8. The rooms were empty, but they wore a look of expectancy.
9. The leaves fairly danced across the page of Jane's autumn drawing.
10. The thunder cracked its mighty whip across the sky as the lightning sped through the air.

Character, Setting, Plot: Write a short phrase or sentence to answer each question.

1. What does the term "character" mean? ______________________________

____

2. Name the members of the Moffat family. Who is the oldest child? Who is the youngest? ________

____

____

3. What does the term "setting" mean? ______________________________

____

4. What is the setting of *The Moffats*? In what region of the country is the imaginary town of Cranbury located? ______________________________

____

5. What does the term "plot" mean? ______________________________

____

____

Multiple Choice: Circle the letter of the BEST answer.

1. What is Mama's occupation?

   a. a dance teacher

   b. an art teacher

   c. a house cleaner

   d. a dressmaker (a seamstress)

2. Who is Madame, and what purpose does she serve?

   a. She is Mama's boss and tells Mama what to do.

   b. She is a dressmaker's dummy and can mimic anyone's body.

   c. She is an assistant to the chief of police who tells him to look for Jane.

   d. She is the Moffats' pet cat.

3. How does meeting Mr. Pennypepper affect Jane's day?

   a. Jane is worried he will tell her to go to school.

   b. Jane is happy to meet someone new and invites him to meet her family.

   c. Jane is afraid she will be arrested because she mimicked his interesting walk.

   d. Jane is disappointed because he wants to sell her house.

4. What is the positive outcome of the boys' train adventure?

   a. The experience on the train makes Hughie want to go to school so he can become an engineer.

   b. There was a kind man who helped the boys return home.

   c. They returned home so late that they did not have to return to school.

   d. The teacher never noticed that they were missing.

5. How do the Moffats justify their Sunday adventure as a good deed?

   a. They reason that the Salvation Army is just like Sunday school.

   b. They see that the man is tired and that they can let him rest.

   c. They think that helping the man is better than being late for Sunday school.

   d. all of the above

6. What is the second sign on the yellow house? Why is it there?

   a. Free Kittens; Catherine had new kittens.

   b. Quarantine; Rufus has scarlet fever.

   c. Vote for Dr. Witty; Dr. Witty is running for mayor of Cranbury.

   d. New Lower Price; The yellow house has not been sold yet.

7. What is Mama's reaction to the news that Joe and Jane have lost the money?

   a. She is calm and understanding. She tries to make the best of it.

   b. She thinks of ways for Joe to earn money to make up for what he has lost.

   c. She is irate and sends them to bed with no supper.

   d. She stares at them in disbelief.

8. How does Jane break the Moffats' sharing code?

   a. She buys caramels for each of her siblings.

   b. She saves her nickel instead of spending it on something for her siblings.

   c. She spends her nickel on an ice cream cone for herself.

   d. She gives her nickel to Mr. Brooney's daughter.

9. How do the Murdocks become involved with the Moffats?

   a. Their daughter, Letitia, is a good friend of Jane's.

   b. Mrs. Murdock asks Mama to sew a dress for her.

   c. They notice the yellow house while Jane is cleaning mud off of the "For Sale" sign.

   d. Mr. Murdock inspects the Moffats' roof for leaks.

10. Why does Rufus want to ride the Second Avenue trolley?

   a. He is tired and does not want to walk to the beach.

   b. He has never ridden a trolley before.

   c. He wants to see if he can ride the trolley for free.

   d. He wants to learn about becoming a motorman.

Short Answer

Answer the following questions in complete sentences.

1. List two differences in activities and surroundings that you have noticed between the Moffats' life and your own. ______________________

2. How do Sylvie, Jane, and Joe each feel about dancing lessons? ______________________

3. Describe two ways the Moffats try to save money. ______________________

4. Give one example of Jane's overactive imagination. ______________________

5. Describe how the Moffats' new house is different from the yellow house. ______________________

Paragraph

Write a paragraph (at least five sentences) about your favorite character in *The Moffats*. Include an introductory sentence and a concluding sentence. Explain why you like this character best.

Quizzes & Final Test Key

The Moffats Quiz 1
Chapters 1-6

Name ____________________

Date ____________________

Write the letter of the vocabulary word on the line in front of its definition.

1. c to mimic		a. viaduct
2. f aggressively		b. subdued
3. e leisurely strolled		c. impersonate
4. h in full agreement		d. pensive
5. i supplies		e. sauntered
6. j moving uncontrollably		f. belligerently
7. d thoughtful		g. contempt
8. a bridge		h. unanimous
9. g dislike; disapproval		i. provisions
10. b quiet; restrained		j. careening

Match each name below with the character description.

Jane	**Capt. Salvation Army**	**Hughie Pudge**	**Mr. Allgood**	**Mr. Pennypepper**
Peter Frost	**Miss Chichester**	**Mama**	**Madame**	**Chief Mulligan**

1. Miss Chichester — told Joe his impromptu performance made a success of the recital
2. Mama — works as a seamstress for a living
3. Mr. Allgood — causes the children to sit as straight as ramrods
4. Jane — likes to look at things the upside-down way
5. Capt. of the Salvation Army — could only be awakened by the beat of a drum
6. Madame — used as a model for Mama's customers
7. Hughie Pudge — decided to become an engineer when he grows up.
8. Chief Mulligan — laughed so hard that tears ran into his whiskers
9. Peter Frost — an insufferable bully
10. Mr. Pennypepper — nods politely to everyone he passes

Choose the **best** answer for each question.

1. What is Mama's occupation?
   (a.) a dressmaker
   b. a dance teacher
   c. an art teacher
   d. a house cleaner

2. Who is Madame, and what purpose does she serve?
   a. She is Mama's boss and tells Mama what to do.
   (b.) She is a dressmaker's dummy and can mimic anyone's body.
   c. She is an assistant to the chief of police who tells him to look for Jane.
   d. She is the Moffats' pet cat.

3. How does meeting Mr. Pennypepper affect Jane's day?
   a. Jane is worried he will tell her to go to school.
   (b.) Jane is afraid she will be arrested because she mimics his interesting walk.
   c. Jane is happy to meet someone new and invites him to meet her family.
   d. Jane is disappointed because he wants to sell her house.

4. What was the positive outcome of the boys' train adventure?
   a. There was a kind man who helped the boys return home.
   b. They returned home so late that they did not have to return to school.
   (c.) The experience on the train makes Hughie want to go to school so he can become an engineer.
   d. The teacher never noticed that they were missing.

5. How do the Moffats justify their Sunday adventure as a good deed?
   a. They reason that the Salvation Army is just like Sunday school.
   b. They see that the man is tired and that they can let him rest.
   c. They think that helping the man is better than being late for Sunday school.
   (d.) all of the above

Answer the following questions in complete sentences.

1. List two differences in activities and surroundings that you have noticed between the Moffats' life and your own.

Rufus plays marbles, an airplane flying overhead is an unusual event, Jane knits, they have a potbellied stove, Mama makes dresses for a living, the For Sale sign is nailed directly to the house, there is a hitching post, and trolleys are a common way to travel.

2. How do Mr. Pennypepper's instructions conflict with Mama's instructions?

Mama had told Rufus to wait at school for Jane; she had also told the children never to go onto the railroad tracks. Mr. Pennypepper tells Rufus to bring Hughie back if he runs away from school. He wants Rufus to watch out for Hughie.

3. List two grudges the Moffats had against Peter Frost.

Peter pulls Sylvie's curls, he made Rufus fall off the hitching post, he tricked Jane and put sand in her mouth, and he scared Jane into thinking she could be arrested for mimicking someone.

4. Who lived in the yellow house before the Moffats? What was his occupation?

Dr. Witty had lived in the house. He was a dentist.

5. How do Sylvie, Jane, and Joe each feel about dancing lessons?

Sylvie: Sylvie loves her dance lessons and has a natural talent for it.

Jane: Jane likes to imagine herself as a graceful dancer, but actually isn't a good dancer.

Joe: Joe dislikes lessons very much, isn't any good, and tries to avoid them.

The Moffats Quiz 2
Chapters 7-12

Name ______________________

Date ______________________

Write the letter of the vocabulary word on the line in front of its definition.

1. ___i___ enemies; competitors	a. protruded
2. ___d___ comfort	b. inopportune
3. ___e___ unconcerned; uninterested	c. aghast
4. ___g___ passionately; zealously	d. consolation
5. ___c___ shocked; dismayed	e. indifferent
6. ___j___ threateningly	f. implored
7. ___h___ scornful	g. fervently
8. ___f___ urgently begged	h. disdainful
9. ___a___ extended	i. adversaries
10. ___b___ inconvenient	j. menacingly

Match each name below with the character description.

Joe	**motorman McCann**	**Sylvie**	**Letitia Murdock**	**motorman O'Brien**
Boots	**Tilly Cadwalader**	**Jane**	**Rufus**	**Dr. Belknap**

1. ___Sylvie___ spends the first week of summer vacation at Camp Lincoln
2. ___Dr. Belknap___ a good, jolly man who diagnoses Rufus' scarlet fever
3. ___Joe___ practices his stilt-walking in the backyard
4. ___Tilly Cadwalader___ the only girl in her family that wears her hair high on her head
5. ___Rufus___ wanted to ride the trolley to see the business about the red lights
6. ___Boots___ shows marks of personality that lift her above the usual run of cats and kittens
7. ___Jane___ was a pig, that's what, a pig
8. ___Letitia Murdock___ would ring the doorbell, then run to the back door and knock
9. ___motorman O'Brien___ wears his hat tipped on his head and sits all slouchy on his stool
10. ___motorman McCann___ an old man who takes driving a trolley car very seriously

Choose the **best** answer for each question.

1. What is the second sign on the yellow house? Why is it there?
   a. Free Kittens!; Catherine had new kittens.
   (b.) Quarantine; Rufus has scarlet fever.
   c. New Lower Price; The yellow house has not been sold yet.
   d. Vote for Dr. Witty; Dr. Witty is running for mayor of Cranbury.

2. What is Mama's reaction to the news that Joe and Jane have lost the money to buy coal?
   a. She is irate and sends them to bed with no supper.
   (b.) She is calm and understanding. She tries to make the best of it.
   c. She thinks of ways for Joe to earn money to make up for what he has lost.
   d. She stares at them in disbelief.

3. How does Jane break the Moffat's sharing code?
   a. She buys caramels for each of her siblings.
   b. She saves her nickel instead of spending it on something for her siblings.
   (c.) She spends her nickel on an ice cream cone for herself.
   d. She gives her nickel to Mr. Brooney's daughter.

4. How do the Murdocks become involved with the Moffats?
   a. Their daughter, Letitia, is a good friend of Jane's.
   (b.) They notice the yellow house while Jane is cleaning mud off of the For Sale sign.
   c. Mrs. Murdock asks Mama to sew a dress for her.
   d. Mr. Murdock inspects the Moffats' roof for leaks.

5. Why does Rufus want to ride the Second Avenue trolley?
   a. He is tired and does not want to walk to the beach.
   b. He has never ridden a trolley before.
   c. He wants to see if he can ride the trolley for free.
   (d.) He wants to learn about becoming a motorman.

Answer the following questions in complete sentences.

1. Give one example of how illness is treated differently in the Moffats' time compared to today's methods. Some specific differences would be that the Moffats are quarantined in the house, the doctor visits Rufus in their home rather than at his office, and a grocery boy comes to their house to deliver groceries.

2. Describe two ways the Moffats try to save money.
Jane puts cardboard inside her shoe where the sole has worn away. Joe sifts through the ashes to find lumps of coal they can reburn. Mama manages the money very carefully, and she tells Joe to count the change carefully.

3. Describe an example of Jane's overactive imagination. Give details.
Ch. 2 - While in the bread box she pictures herself as a princess locked in a cavern.
Ch. 5 - Jane is frightened by the ghost she helped to build.
Ch. 6 - She imagines herself to be a graceful dancer.
Ch. 7 - She imagines she is the little match girl.
Ch. 9 - She imagines the horse has wings, is the wooden horse of Troy, and is a bridge.

4. What excitement is encountered on the trolley?
Two trolleys run in opposite directions on the same track, and one is supposed to wait for the other to complete its run. However, the motorman driving the Moffats' trolley decides to confront the other motorman and there is almost a crash as the two trolleys meet on the track.

5. Describe how the Moffats' new house is different from the yellow house.
The new house is smaller with a huge front yard and a small backyard. It has few trees and only one arbor. However, they know that eventually there might be many things they will like.

The Moffats Final Test

Name ______________________

Date ______________________

Vocabulary: Write the letter of the vocabulary word next to its definition.

1. g supplies
2. b to mimic
3. j dislike; disapproval
4. d in full agreement
5. f thoughtful
6. i aggressively
7. a scornful
8. e enemies; competitors
9. c urgently begged
10. h unconcerned; uninterested

a. disdainful
b. impersonate
c. implored
d. unanimous
e. adversaries
f. pensive
g. provisions
h. indifferent
i. belligerently
j. contempt

Character Identification: Choose the name that matches each description and write it on the line.

Mr. Allgood	Letitia Murdock	Jane	Peter Frost	Chief Mulligan
Rufus	Miss Chichester	Joe	Mama	Boots

1. Miss Chichester — told Joe his impromptu performance made a success of the recital
2. Mr. Allgood — causes the children to sit as straight as ramrods
3. Jane — likes to look at things the upside-down way
4. Chief Mulligan — laughed so hard that tears ran into his whiskers
5. Peter Frost — an insufferable bully
6. Joe — practices his stilt walking in the backyard
7. Rufus — wanted to ride the trolley to see the business about the red lights
8. Boots — shows marks of personality that lift her above the usual run of cats and kittens
9. Letitia Murdock — would ring and ring the doorbell, then run around to the back door and knock
10. Mama — works as a seamstress for a living

Personification: Circle the noun that is being personified. Underline the words that show human characteristics.

1. The freighters in the train yard beckoned to him invitingly until he could resist no longer.
2. But the wind was now on their backs and urged them up the street swiftly.
3. The wind tried to snatch their hats from their heads.
4. Madame was on the porch wearing a rather disapproving air.
5. The engine of the Bay State Express was just itching to be off.
6. The longer she stared at it the louder the sign screamed that this was no longer her house.
7. In her imagination Jane's feet carefully followed each step of the dance with graceful ease.
8. The rooms were empty, but they wore a look of expectancy.
9. The leaves fairly danced across the page of Jane's autumn drawing.
10. The thunder cracked its mighty whip across the sky as the lightning sped through the air.

Character, Setting, Plot: Write a short phrase or sentence to answer each question.

1. What does the term "character" mean? The characters are the main people in the story. They are who the story is about.
2. Name the members of the Moffat family. Who is the oldest child? Who is the youngest? The Moffat family consists of Mama, Sylvie, Joe, Jane, and Rufus. Sylvie is the oldest child and Rufus is the youngest.
3. What does the term "setting" mean? The setting tells the time and place in which the story takes place.
4. What is the setting of *The Moffats*? In what region of the country is the imaginary town of Cranbury located? The setting of the Moffats is in the early 1900s. It takes place in the New England area of the U.S., specifically in Connecticut.
5. What does the term "plot" mean? The plot is the action of the story, or what actually takes place in the story.

Multiple Choice: Circle the letter of the BEST answer.

1. What is Mama's occupation?
   a. a dance teacher
   b. an art teacher
   c. a house cleaner
   (d.) a dressmaker (a seamstress)

2. Who is Madame, and what purpose does she serve?
   a. She is Mama's boss and tells Mama what to do.
   (b.) She is a dressmaker's dummy and can mimic anyone's body.
   c. She is an assistant to the chief of police who tells him to look for Jane.
   d. She is the Moffats' pet cat.

3. How does meeting Mr. Pennypepper affect Jane's day?
   a. Jane is worried he will tell her to go to school.
   b. Jane is happy to meet someone new and invites him to meet her family.
   (c.) Jane is afraid she will be arrested because she mimicked his interesting walk.
   d. Jane is disappointed because he wants to sell her house.

4. What is the positive outcome of the boys' train adventure?
   (a.) The experience on the train makes Hughie want to go to school so he can become an engineer.
   b. There was a kind man who helped the boys return home.
   c. They returned home so late that they did not have to return to school.
   d. The teacher never noticed that they were missing.

5. How do the Moffats justify their Sunday adventure as a good deed?
   a. They reason that the Salvation Army is just like Sunday school.
   b. They see that the man is tired and that they can let him rest.
   c. They think that helping the man is better than being late for Sunday school.
   (d.) all of the above

6. What is the second sign on the yellow house? Why is it there?

a. Free Kittens; Catherine had new kittens.

(b.) Quarantine; Rufus has scarlet fever.

c. Vote for Dr. Witty; Dr. Witty is running for mayor of Cranbury.

d. New Lower Price; The yellow house has not been sold yet.

7. What is Mama's reaction to the news that Joe and Jane have lost the money?

(a.) She is calm and understanding. She tries to make the best of it.

b. She thinks of ways for Joe to earn money to make up for what he has lost.

c. She is irate and sends them to bed with no supper.

d. She stares at them in disbelief.

8. How does Jane break the Moffats' sharing code?

a. She buys caramels for each of her siblings.

b. She saves her nickel instead of spending it on something for her siblings.

(c.) She spends her nickel on an ice cream cone for herself.

d. She gives her nickel to Mr. Brooney's daughter.

9. How do the Murdocks become involved with the Moffats?

a. Their daughter, Letitia, is a good friend of Jane's.

b. Mrs. Murdock asks Mama to sew a dress for her.

(c.) They notice the yellow house while Jane is cleaning mud off of the "For Sale" sign.

d. Mr. Murdock inspects the Moffats' roof for leaks.

10. Why does Rufus want to ride the Second Avenue trolley?

a. He is tired and does not want to walk to the beach.

b. He has never ridden a trolley before.

c. He wants to see if he can ride the trolley for free.

(d.) He wants to learn about becoming a motorman.

Short Answer

Answer the following questions in complete sentences.

1. List two differences in activities and surroundings that you have noticed between the Moffats' life and your own. Rufus plays marbles, an airplane flying overhead is an unusual event, Jane knits, they have a potbellied stove, Mama makes dresses for a living, the For Sale sign is nailed directly to the house, there is a hitching post, and trolleys are a common way to travel.

2. How do Sylvie, Jane, and Joe each feel about dancing lessons?
   Sylvie loves her dance lessons and has a natural talent for it.
   Jane likes to imagine herself as a graceful dancer, but actually isn't a good dancer.
   Joe dislikes lessons very much, isn't any good, and tries to avoid them.

3. Describe two ways the Moffats try to save money. Jane puts cardboard inside her shoe where the sole has worn away. Joe sifts through the ashes to find lumps of coal they can reburn. Mama manages the money very carefully, and she tells Joe to count the change carefully.

4. Give one example of Jane's overactive imagination. Possible answers: While in the bread box she pictures herself as a princess locked in a cavern; Jane is frightened by the ghost she helped to build; she imagines herself to be a graceful dancer; she imagines she is the little match girl; she imagines the horse has wings, is the wooden horse of Troy, and is a bridge.

5. Describe how the Moffats' new house is different from the yellow house.
   The new house is smaller with a huge front yard and a small backyard. It has few trees and only one arbor. However, they know that eventually there might be many things they will like.

Paragraph

Write a paragraph (at least five sentences) about your favorite character in *The Moffats*. Include an introductory sentence and a concluding sentence. Explain why you like this character best.